CONTENTS

DIRECTOR'S FOREWORD

The question of what makes a great photographic portrait is generally considered to be a subjective matter. A location, individual (or group) and pose that affects one person deeply may hold little interest or charm for another. As photographs for the *Taylor Wessing Photographic Portrait Prize* are viewed by the jury, it may be a unanimous view that takes a portrait through to the second round, or the opinion of a single judge who is intrigued or impressed. During the second round, that engagement may grow with the enthusiasm of the rest of the jury, and a shared sense of the importance of the portrait will emerge in the final selection. The collective outcome will cover works as diverse as perfectly poised subjects on location, documentary portraits capturing a particular moment and highly charged images of personal tragedy or joy, many with narrative elements that may or may not be fully explained.

While some competitions understandably opt for digital submission, we remain keen for our judges to see the print from the start. Judging the prints (which is done anonymously) places great stress on the printing of the photograph as well as the composition of the image. Only from prints can the richness and subtlety of the very best portraits be appreciated to the full.

I am very grateful to the many photographers who submitted 6,033 images to the *Taylor Wessing Photographic Portrait Prize* 2011. Many congratulations go to this year's winners: Jooney Woodward, Jill Wooster, Dona Schwartz, Jasper Clarke (who is also the *ELLE* Commission winner) and David Knight. I am also grateful to Lorraine Candy, Editor, and her colleagues at *ELLE* magazine for the collaboration through which selected photographers are featured in the magazine and one is offered a commission to make new work.

I should like to thank my fellow judges: Monica Allende, Michael Bracewell, Venetia Dearden, Clare Ferguson and Terence Pepper. Thanks also to National Portrait Gallery staff, the designers Thomas Manss & Company and the interviewer Richard McClure for their hard work on the exhibition and the catalogue. I am grateful again to The White Wall Company for their expert contribution to the logistical management of the submission and judging process.

My special thanks go to Taylor Wessing and to Tim Eyles, UK Managing Partner. The continuing partnership grows in strength each year and is hugely appreciated by the Gallery, and by the public in their enjoyment of the prize and the exhibition.

SANDY NAIRNE
DIRECTOR, NATIONAL PORTRAIT GALLERY

SPONSOR'S FOREWORD

At Taylor Wessing we are delighted to continue our relationship with the National Portrait Gallery. In our fourth year of supporting the *Photographic Portrait Prize*, we have found ourselves once again inspired by the outstanding talent and vision of the entrants.

As ever, the submissions have an international flavour, capturing the diverse experiences of photographers the world over. This year's exhibition radiates a particularly strong sense of social commentary, with many works addressing both the difficulties and the celebrations experienced by ordinary people throughout the world today. It is their sense of realism and depth of vision that makes the images both relevant and easy to relate to. These portraits do not merely offer insight, but provoke questions and catalyse debates, their art often bringing uncomfortable issues to the surface.

Taylor Wessing is proud to be strongly committed to supporting arts and culture. This competition in particular correlates with our own values: its encouragement and cultivation of new talent alongside that of established professionals; the wonderful diversity of images that evoke such varied reactions; and the far-reaching nature of the competition on a geographic level, attracting entries of the highest quality from across the globe.

At Taylor Wessing we always find this exhibition truly inspiring, not only because of the photographs themselves, but also because working alongside the National Portrait Gallery gives us the opportunity to add another dimension to the work we do with our charity partners, in particular St Mungo's, a charity that opens doors for homeless people. Bringing the two together allows us to run art initiatives, such as photography workshops, for individuals who would not otherwise have access to the arts. It is a true privilege to be able to help inject some colour and light into the lives of others. We are also exploring our artistic side with our other charity partner, Kids Company. Kids Company uses art as a tool of communication and therapy, and we look forward to exploring how we can bring our relationships with the Gallery and Kids Company together to develop that.

I hope that you will share our enjoyment of the works from this year's *Taylor Wessing Photographic Portrait Prize* and join in congratulating all those who have helped to create yet another fascinating and successful exhibition, as well as each and every entrant. I would also like to thank the National Portrait Gallery, and look forward to continuing our partnership over the coming years.

TIM EYLES
MANAGING PARTNER, TAYLOR WESSING LLP

TaylorWessing

CREATING A VISUAL AUTOGRAPH
MICHAEL BRACEWELL

I have never sat for a formal photographic portrait, nor attempted to take a serious photograph of anyone else. But the four published volumes of Richard Hamilton's *Polaroid Portraits* have always struck me as a near-perfect engagement with the form.

The great pioneer of Pop Art would ask friends and acquaintances to take his picture with a Polaroid camera – the result being a collection of what might be termed 'visual autographs'. Each Polaroid portrait of Hamilton becomes, perhaps unsurprisingly, a portrait of the person who took the photograph. Bryan Ferry, for example, lights and poses his former tutor in the sumptuous, bronze-lit style of a Rembrandt painting; Derek Jarman – the subject of one of Hamilton's own portraits – renders the Polaroid image a near-Cubist shudder of ghostly forms; Peter Blake, by contrast, snaps Hamilton in conversation with the singer Ian Dury: together, a pair of Pop Art's coolest operators.

As a huge admirer of Hamilton's art and ideas, I have often wondered what my own Polaroid autograph would have looked like, were the great man ever to have invited me to make his photographic portrait. Would I have simply adopted a 'point and shoot' approach and hoped for the best, or would I have attempted to style my subject? Most probably, I would have asked Hamilton to hold a copy of *The Beatles* (the so-called *White Album*), for which he conceived and designed the iconic packaging. Or, given that the first eight million copies of *The Beatles* were stamped with an edition number (Hamilton took number 0000000, and the Beatles themselves took the first four), I would have perhaps attempted to take a bleached-out 'white' Polaroid and stamp it with a serial number.

These ponderings remain in the realm of fantasy, but one sultry morning in the summer of 1979 I did manage to take an all-white Polaroid. I was standing in a queue in the old Arts Council bookshop – then on Long Acre, in Covent Garden – attempting with sweating hands to take a Polaroid photograph of the other great pioneer of Pop, Andy Warhol. The occasion was a public signing of his book *Exposures* – in retrospect a rather sickly volume, containing page after page of black-and-white photographs of soft-skinned, beaming – but clearly ruthless – international socialites. Thirty-three years later, the book is of interest, since it tracks Warhol's move into a form of cultural anaesthesia, in which a parade of names and money assumes the air of mass-produced consumer products or machine parts. (Which isn't to say that Warhol didn't enjoy the parties and the glamour.)

Twenty years old, aspiring to the pale and interesting fringes of post-punk, I stood with all the other punk youngsters waiting to breathe the same air as the man who had apparently invented us all – who, by using cheap media, had proclaimed us all to be stars (however perverse) and all beauties (however obscure). Several large, black cars pulled up outside the bookshop, and immediately the situation turned into the publicity equivalent of a gunfight in the saloon of a Western. Everyone started photographing everybody else (an act of premonition, in hindsight), regardless, it seemed, of who they were. Order was restored, the queue reformed, and some hours later, authorised by the whispered syllable, 'Sure', I took my Polaroid of Andy Warhol. It came out blank – a dull, neon white – which sort of made sense.

THE PRIZES

TAYLOR WESSING PHOTOGRAPHIC PORTRAIT PRIZE

The *Taylor Wessing Photographic Portrait Prize* is open to photographers from around the world aged eighteen or over.

The first prize winner is Jooney Woodward, who receives £12,000.

The second prize winner is Jill Wooster, who receives £2,500.

The third prize winner is Dona Schwartz, who receives £1,500.

The fourth prize winner is Jasper Clarke, who receives £1,000.

The fifth prize winner is David Knight, who receives £500.

THE *ELLE* COMMISSION

The *ELLE* Commission winner is selected by the magazine's creative director, Marissa Bourke, along with *ELLE*'s art director, Tom Meredith, and picture editor, Flora Bathurst, to shoot a feature story for the magazine.

The winner is Jasper Clarke.

If you would like to join the mailing list to receive an entry form for next year's *Photographic Portrait Prize*, please register your interest online at: www.npg.org.uk/photoprize or send your full contact details to:

Photographic Portrait Prize 2012
Marketing Department
National Portrait Gallery
St Martin's Place
London WC2H 0HE

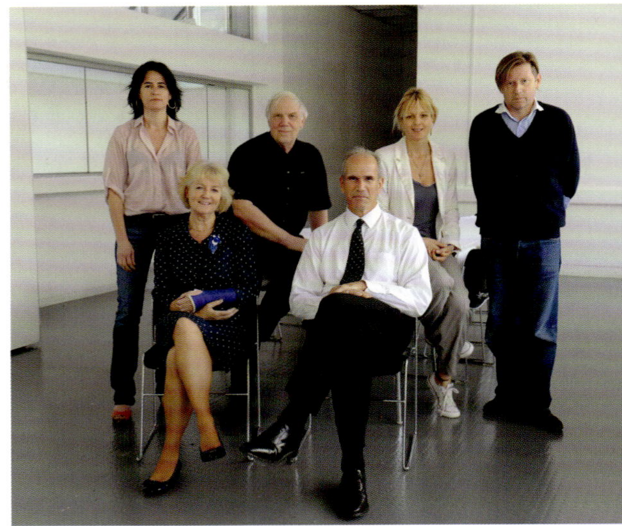

PHOTOGRAPH BY VENETIA DEARDEN

THE JUDGES, CLOCKWISE FROM LEFT: MONICA ALLENDE, TERENCE PEPPER, VENETIA DEARDEN, MICHAEL BRACEWELL, SANDY NAIRNE AND CLARE FERGUSON.

THE JUDGES

CHAIR: SANDY NAIRNE

DIRECTOR, NATIONAL PORTRAIT GALLERY

This year's entries for the *Taylor Wessing Photographic Portrait Prize* were as diverse and fascinating as those of previous years, representing the very best in photographic portraits from around the world. Some images reflected current world events; others were timeless reflections of the scrutiny or passion of the particular photographer. Finding the best sixty portraits for the exhibition was a combined process of creative debate, and I am most grateful for the attentive interest of the judges, and to all the photographers who submitted.

MONICA ALLENDE

PICTURE EDITOR, *THE SUNDAY TIMES*

I felt incredibly privileged to be part of the jury for this year's *Taylor Wessing Photographic Portrait Prize*, an award that has been a point of reference throughout my career. Viewing the sheer abundance of imaginative, intelligent and unexpected responses to portraiture felt like being let loose in a sweet shop – not that any decision was taken lightly. Rather, each and every frame provoked dialogue and debate across the panel. It was a truly elevating experience: a rare opportunity to view our times through the eyes of over 6,000 photographers, and a reminder of what an eclectic bunch we humans are!

MICHAEL BRACEWELL

WRITER AND NOVELIST

For anyone interested in visual culture – of almost any sort – the experience of co-judging the *Taylor Wessing Photographic Portrait Prize* would be of profound interest. Due to the phenomenal popularity of the award and accompanying exhibition, there are a large number of entries to be considered and sifted down to potential prizewinners. This process is an extraordinarily intense experience for a judge. All portraits are encoded with an emotional imprint of some sort, and to be exposed to such a concentrated image flow over the course of two days' judging is inevitably demanding. At the same time, one's visual sense becomes increasingly sharpened, and sensitised to recognising those images that immediately interrupt the denser flow, their appeal more visceral than merely aesthetic. Living in a society where we are constantly bombarded by images of all kinds, it is oddly heartening to know that impact and originality remain not only possible, but of increasing value.

VENETIA DEARDEN

PHOTOGRAPHER

If a portrait is a considered conversation between artist and subject, it's fascinating how the language of some images endures and triumphs during two days of dynamic analysis. The selection process was intense, challenging and surprisingly emotional. I found it reassuring that the winners were chosen from finalists selected unanimously, some of which we all became quite attached to by championing them on this journey. Judging the *Taylor Wessing Photographic Portrait Prize* is a responsibility and an inspiration, and I feel positive that the resulting exhibition reflects the strengths and diversity of contemporary portrait photography.

CLARE FERGUSON

CONSULTANT, TAYLOR WESSING LLP

I was delighted to be part of the judging panel this year and found the process enthralling, impressive and exciting, as well as demanding. Every portrait is given close attention and, during the day, one photograph may lose favour after debate and a closer look whereas another will come up quietly on the inside track as its image continues to impress – a photograph that perhaps was not an obvious candidate for prominence at first viewing. Sandy chairs the meeting with impeccable fairness. The fact that the panel is not told the identity of the photographers ensures that each photograph is selected on its own strength. It is a real privilege to assist in this selection process and be shown images from around the world, recording life with all its variety and vicissitudes. Such is the concentration required that long after the judging ended many images remain in my memory, and I hope they have the same effect on all who visit the exhibition.

TERENCE PEPPER

CURATOR OF PHOTOGRAPHS, NATIONAL PORTRAIT GALLERY

Each week I view thousands of images in printed media and on the Internet, but judging the annual *Taylor Wessing Photographic Portrait Prize* entries is a visual highlight of my year – a golden opportunity to view, over two intense days of judging, the most remarkable selections of portraits submitted from all corners of the world. Year upon year the overall quality of the works entered seems to rise, and reducing the 6,000-plus entries to the sixty finalists is a real test of strength. Happily, each year a newly recruited guest jury, well-versed in contemporary visual culture, allows for a wide cross-section of intriguing, insightful, stimulating and surprising images to make the final cut.

FIRST PRIZE
JOONEY WOODWARD

Jooney Woodward, recipient of the 2011 *Taylor Wessing Photographic Portrait Prize*, took her winning image while scouting for potential subject matter among the sheepdog trials, regimental bands and champion livestock at the Royal Welsh Agricultural Show in Builth Wells, Powys. Woodward encountered thirteen-year-old Harriet Power and her guinea pig, a pink-eyed golden cavy called Gentleman Jack, while the teenager was volunteering as a steward in the judging enclosure.

'I was most struck by the visual potential of Harriet's red hair and the similar colouring of the guinea pig,' recalls Woodward. 'There is a youthfulness about Harriet, but there is also something quite confident and adult about her. I didn't have much time to consider the pose because the judging tables were so hectic, but thankfully I got the shot I wanted in the first frame.'

Woodward shot the portrait on film with a Mamiya RZ medium-format camera on a tripod, using natural light from a skylight. 'I prefer the quality and depth you get from using film; unfortunately, it's a dying art. I don't mess around with Photoshop, so what you see is what you get. Enhanced images can portray a false sense of reality, whereas my work celebrates the people and places as they appear every day.'

Woodward was born in London in 1979 and studied graphic design, specialising in photography, at Camberwell College of Arts, where her degree-show portraits of her parents were highly commended in the *Observer Hodge Photographic Award* in 2001. After graduating, she took a job in the *Vogue* photographic archive of Condé Nast Publications, immersing herself in the work of Cecil Beaton and John Deakin. Leaving to become a freelance photographer in 2009, she travelled throughout Wales, shooting a series of landscapes that were exhibited in her first solo show, *Unhidden*, at the Museum of Modern Art in Machynlleth last year.

'My landscapes are generally devoid of people, but are full of signs of life. I try to capture the little things and it's the same with my portraiture,' she says. 'The more you look at the portrait of Harriet, the more you notice the small details: her nail polish and mascara, the scratch on her hand.'

The portrait of Harriet has inspired Woodward to continue photographing the 'quirky world' of guinea pig enthusiasts, while she is also developing a series based around model railway exhibitions. 'I like subjects that are often overlooked, but which are actually a huge part of some people's lives. I feel I can see things that perhaps other people don't notice, and I'd like to open up these worlds to a wider audience.'

INTERVIEW BY RICHARD MCCLURE

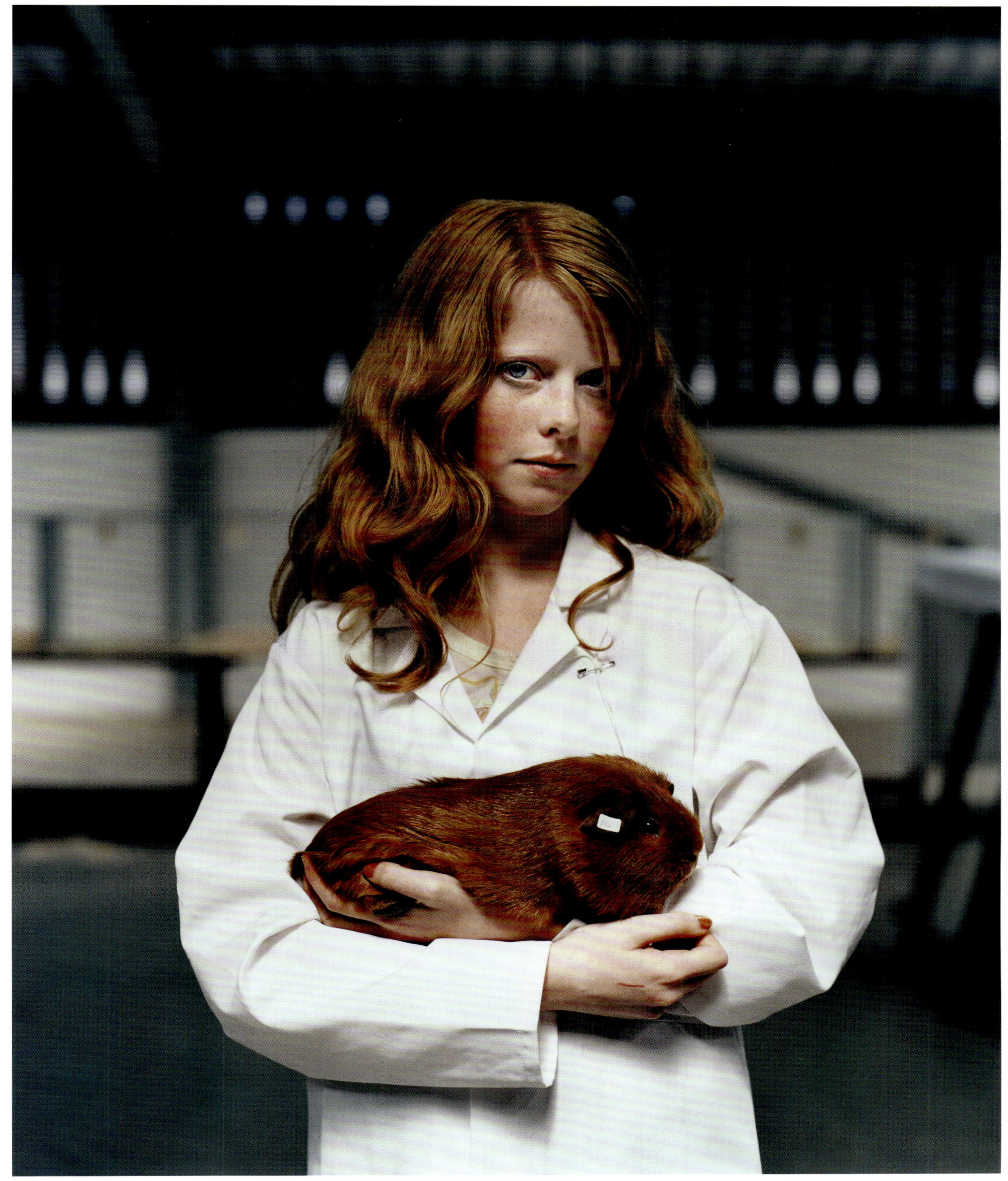

JOONEY WOODWARD
HARRIET AND GENTLEMAN JACK
JULY 2011

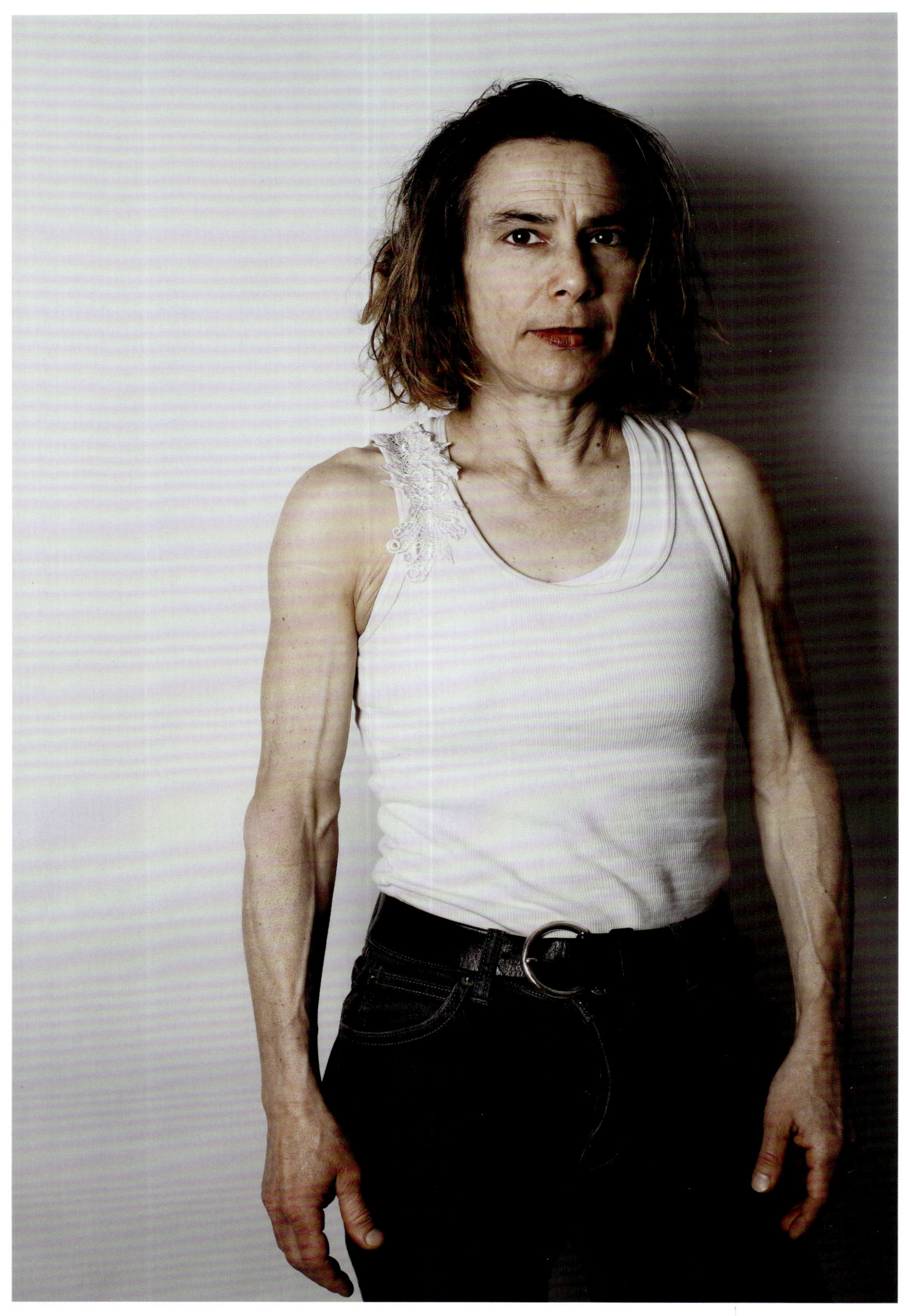

JILL WOOSTER
OF LILI
MAY 2011

SECOND PRIZE
JILL WOOSTER

With the debate surrounding digital retouching continuing to divide photographers, the argument was reignited this year when Mario Testino's portrait of a suspiciously flawless Julia Roberts for a L'Oréal advertising campaign was banned in the UK for breaching standards of exaggeration. American photographer Jill Wooster, however, makes no apology for her own enthusiastic approach towards image manipulation. Wooster specialises in creating highly stylised and manipulated fashion portraits that she characterises as 'over-the-top and slightly surreal'.

'I can see some reasonable objections to retouching images that are billed as photojournalism,' she acknowledges. 'But the roots of the portrait are in painting and painters control and manipulate every aspect of the image they create. Why shouldn't commercial and art photographers do the same? The end result is what counts.'

Born in New Haven, Connecticut in 1977, Wooster studied as an artist, later supplementing her post-college painting career by freelancing as a photographic retoucher, something she still does today. 'It gradually dawned on me that I could approach photography from a painter's perspective, and that's what I'm now trying to achieve – whether by manipulating the image digitally or by carefully planning everything that leads up to the fraction of a second before the shutter clicks. I'm more interested in making pictures than taking them.'

In contrast to the 'obsessive pursuit of perfection' that marks her fashion portfolio, Wooster describes her personal work as 'more introverted, more about an attempt to get under the skin of something'. As such, her portrait *Of Lili* is taken from an ongoing project that portrays middle-aged women at difficult stages in their lives. 'The women are all going through some sort of change. Some are dealing with serious issues such as substance abuse or domestic violence, while others are just dealing with the damage caused by time.'

Wooster, who now lives in London, photographed her friend Lili Ledbetter with a digital single-lens reflex camera during a two-day stay at her Peckham flat. In this instance, the only retouching of the final image was some selective blemish removal.

'Lili lives in San Francisco and is a complicated character,' says Wooster. 'In the portrait, I like the way that her androgyny makes her appearance seem both guarded and relaxed at the same time, which manages to capture both her confidence and her vulnerability. She is a gentle person with, paradoxically, a lot of anger just beneath the surface. I wanted to see if I could capture the balance between those two qualities. I'm not sure I succeeded, but I think I got something else, something even more interesting, which is Lili's strength.'

INTERVIEW BY RICHARD MCCLURE

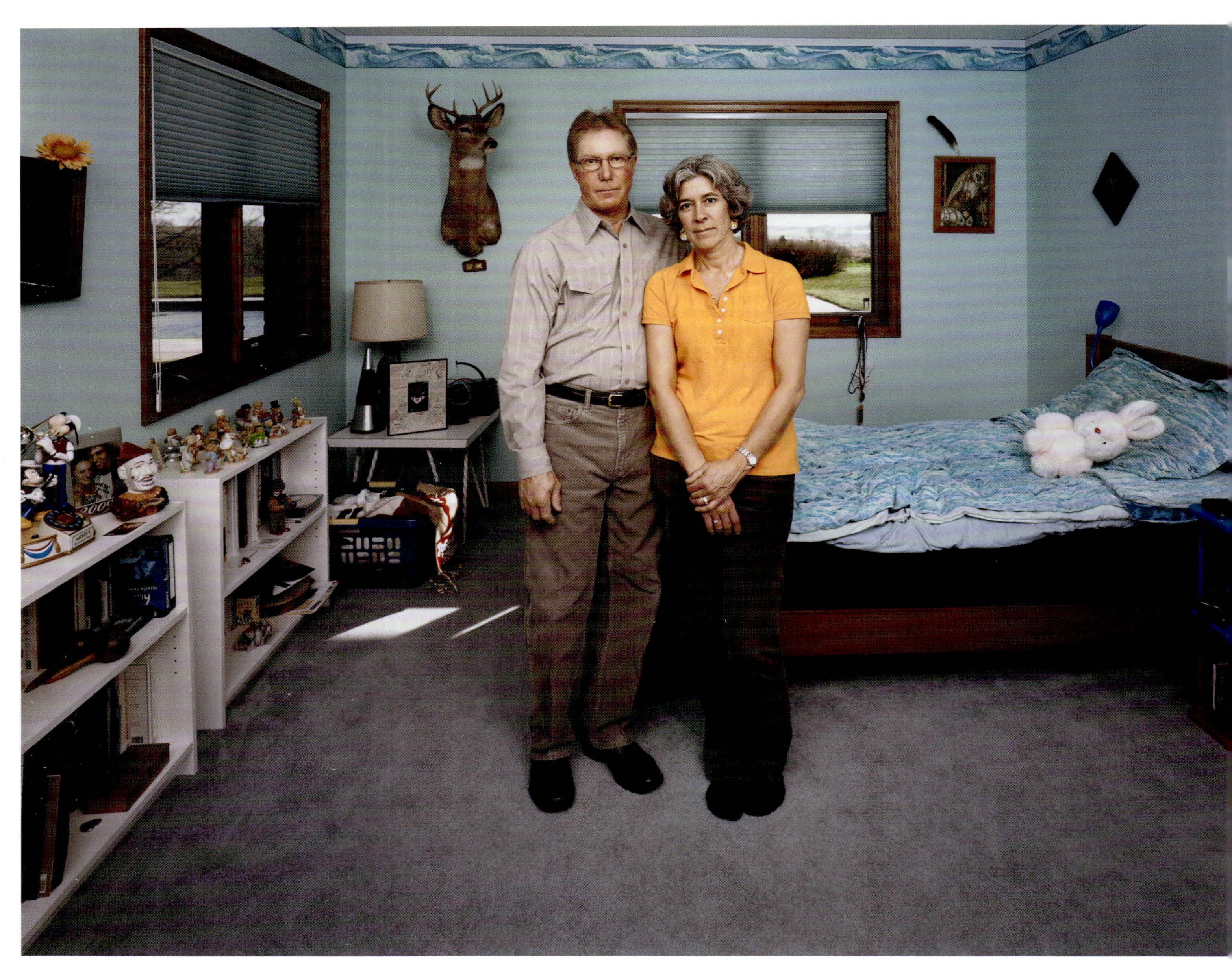

DONA SCHWARTZ
CHRISTINA AND MARK, 14 MONTHS
FROM THE SERIES *ON THE NEST*
NOVEMBER 2010

THIRD PRIZE
DONA SCHWARTZ

While many photographers are drawn to documenting adolescents as they negotiate the often-difficult transition from childhood to adulthood, Dona Schwartz has instead focused her lens on the powerful and conflicting emotions experienced by parents as their teenage children leave the family home.

Her current work-in-progress, *On the Nest*, explores this psychological and physical loss by depicting various parents in the bedrooms once occupied by their departed offspring. Some empty-nesters have wasted no time in turning the spaces into home offices or gyms; others have preserved the rooms as shrines that memorialise the life of the child and the family's history.

'Everyone is fascinated by teenagers, but adults have transitions in their lives too,' explains Schwartz. 'I am interested in how the rooms are used and what they convey about the people who use them. We have rituals for decorating the nursery, but no real ritual for taking apart the room after our children have left. A whole history has collapsed into that space. The work is a document of how we get from one place to the next in our lives.'

Her third-placed entry, *Christina and Mark, 14 months*, portrays a doctor and her businessman husband at home in a rural part of Minnesota. The parents of three grown-up children, the couple had been empty-nesters for fourteen months when the portrait was shot.

'I do not direct my subjects to pose in a particular way because I am interested in how they relate to each other, how they occupy the space, and how they wish to be seen,' says Schwartz. 'I only ask that they look directly at the camera lens because I want the viewer of the portrait to be engaged by their gazes.'

Schwartz is an associate professor at the School of Journalism and Mass Communication at the University of Minnesota, and her earliest publications, including a black-and-white study of an Iowa farming town, were produced from a social scientist's perspective. However, her most recent work has marked a significant shift, both conceptually and visually.

'For many years my images were addressed to an academic audience, but working as an artist has now given me the freedom to experiment,' she explains. 'I was very much a "decisive moment" photographer, but for this project I learned to use 5x4 and studio lights. It's a much more deliberative process and I'm glad I challenged myself to make pictures in a new and different way.'

Schwartz recently became an empty-nester herself when her daughter packed her bags for college, and she plans to complete *On the Nest* in the coming months with a self-portrait. 'I'm sure I'll be sneaking into my daughter's closet to use some of that space,' she predicts. 'I used to think that being an empty-nester would be the most wonderful thing in the world. Now I am not so sure. You are getting your life back, but it is a whole different life.'

INTERVIEW BY RICHARD MCCLURE

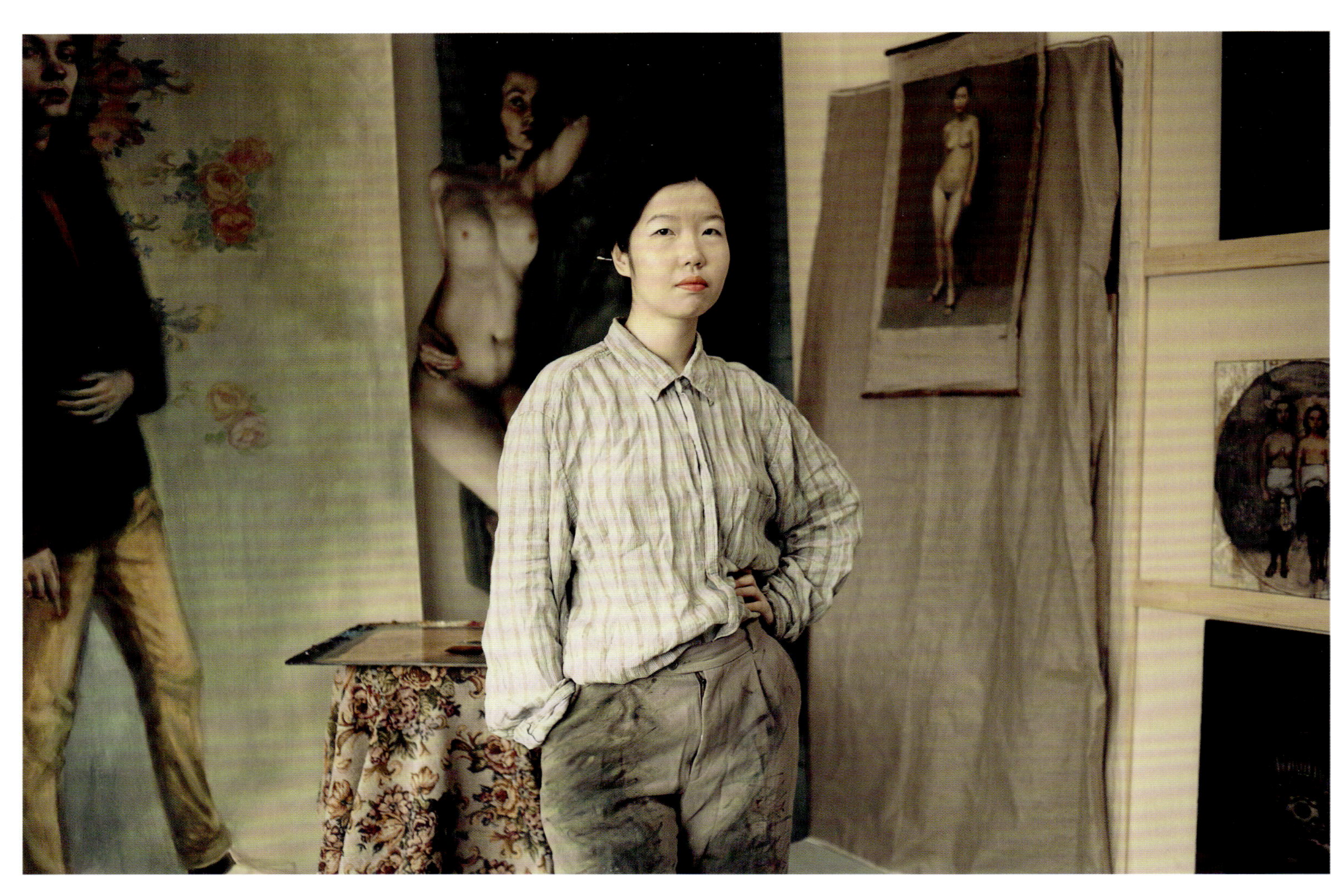

JASPER CLARKE
WEN
MARCH 2011

FOURTH PRIZE AND *ELLE* COMMISSION
JASPER CLARKE

Jasper Clarke found no shortage of volunteers when he began a personal project depicting artists, musicians and other creatives who have been forced to live in their workspaces in order to make ends meet. The thirty-three-year-old photographer, who shares a studio unit in Hackney, started the series after meeting people who were bedding down in the building in order to save money.

'There is no insulation in the unit so it's freezing cold in winter and boiling hot in summer,' says Clarke. 'The portraits are not intended to elicit sympathy for the cash-strapped artist; they are more a celebration of people's dedication in following a path, no matter what the obstacles. I find their pride and defiance quite inspiring.'

Chinese-born artist Wen Wu, the subject of Clarke's portrait, has had a Vivien Leigh obsession since seeing *Gone with the Wind* as a child, and often paints herself alongside the actress in her art works. 'Wen wanted to pose in this wild green dress, but I insisted on photographing her as a painter in front of her canvases,' he recalls. 'I think the colours and tone of the image really work.'

Leaving school without qualifications in 1991, Clarke spent several years 'in and out of factories, building sites and the dole office'. During this period, he began taking pictures with an Olympus 35mm camera, a present from his father, eventually publishing images of his favourite sport, BMX riding, in various bike magazines.

'Shooting my friends on the BMX circuit helped me realise that I didn't want to be in the studio very much as a photographer. As corny as it sounds, my biggest inspiration is the world outside. I love being outdoors and the feeling of freedom and energy it brings.'

A return to education was curtailed when Clarke dropped out of a photography, film and imaging degree course at Edinburgh's Napier University, and he subsequently moved to London where he assisted several high-profile photographers including Nadav Kander and Liz Collins. Since setting up on his own in 2008, he has produced fashion campaigns for Paul Smith, Converse and Umbro. 'It's only been this year that I have felt I am getting my own style together and feeling quite confident in what I am doing,' he says.

His confidence should be boosted by his fourth-place prize and also by winning this year's *ELLE* Commission, which brings the opportunity to shoot a feature story for the magazine. 'I'd like my career to follow the same path as Nadav Kander's,' he says. 'He shoots these huge commercial campaigns but he is also a renowned artist. You can't pigeonhole him and I love that.'

INTERVIEW BY RICHARD MCCLURE

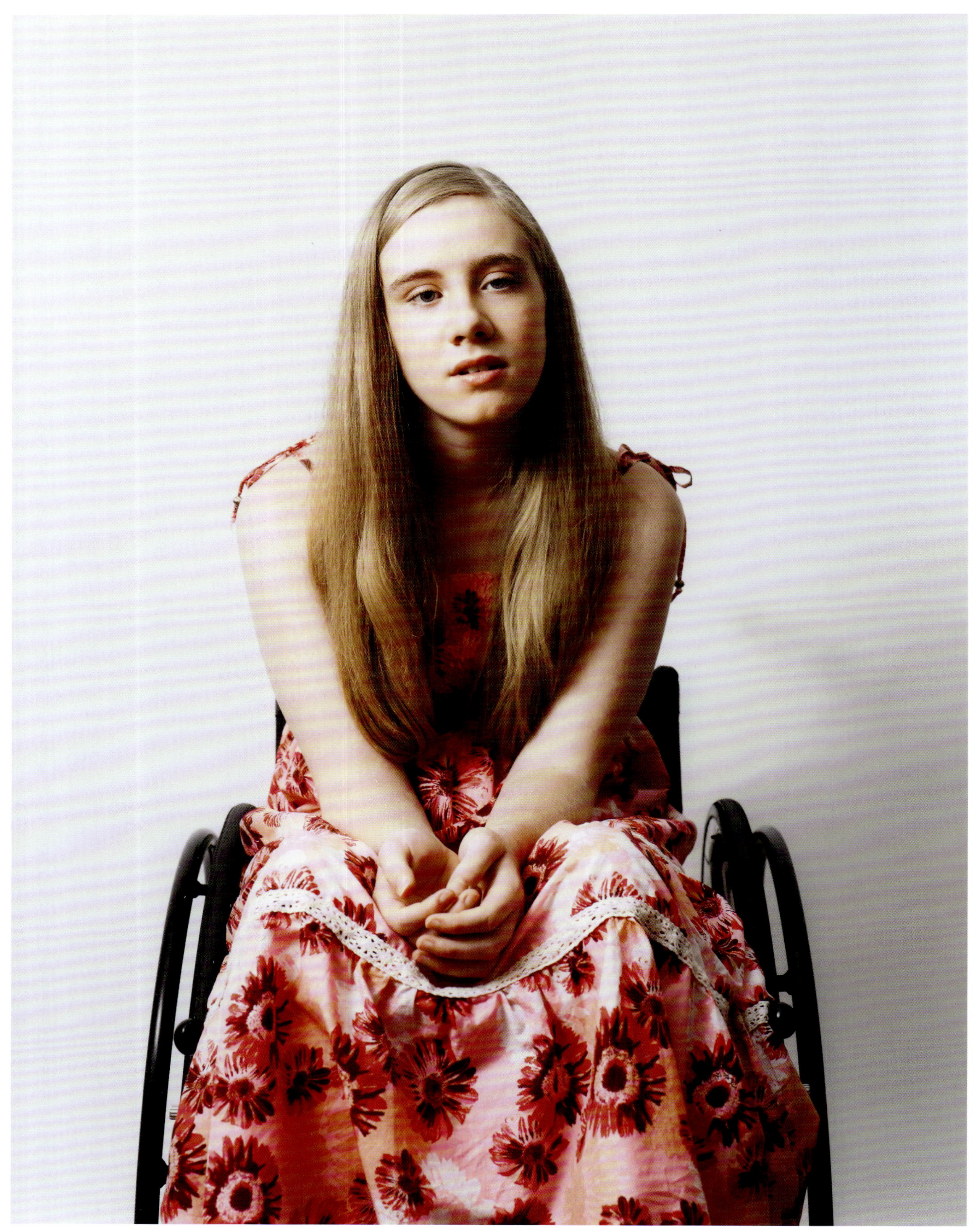

DAVID KNIGHT
ANDIE
FROM THE SERIES *CEREBRAL PALSY AWARENESS*
DECEMBER 2010

FIFTH PRIZE
DAVID KNIGHT

Currently based in Australia, David Knight began his career in his native England where he assisted a number of advertising photographers in London and Oxford before leaving for Dubai in 1995. There, he worked extensively for Saatchi & Saatchi whilst also finding time for other corporate and personal projects, from PR jobs of the region's ruling elite to reportage of Yemeni tribesmen armed with AK-47s.

After four years in the Emirates, Knight moved again, this time relocating to Sydney where he now resides with his wife and twin sons. His commercial portfolio includes advertising campaigns for the likes of Toyota, Visa and Virgin, although in recent years he has consciously devoted more time to his portraiture and people-oriented assignments.

As part of this move, Knight accepted a commission from The Spastic Centre charity which wanted to publicise its name-change to the Cerebral Palsy Alliance and raise awareness of the condition throughout Australia. Knight made a series of ten portraits of children for the campaign, including the picture of Andie Poetschka, a fifteen-year-old with cerebral palsy who lives in Maroubra, New South Wales.

'I wanted the portraits to be positive and to convey the kids in an uplifting way,' says Knight. 'You can't immediately notice Andie is in a wheelchair; you just see this beautiful young woman. The image doesn't demand you look at it, but gently draws you in. It's quietly powerful. Andie struck me as unassuming yet self-assured.'

This is the third year running that Knight's pictures have featured in the *Taylor Wessing Photographic Portrait Prize*. In 2009, a study of his wife's friend Alyssa was selected for exhibition, followed last year by a portrait of model and actress Catharina. 'Both women possess a unique, unconventional beauty,' says Knight. 'I am always drawn to slightly melancholy faces.'

In shooting portraits, Knight says his aim is simplicity and honesty. Most of his sittings are made in a studio environment with controlled lighting. 'A lot of my advertising ventures are finessed in post-production, so I deliberately strip things back in my personal work,' he explains. 'My portraiture is an ongoing project. I am looking constantly to refine my technique to its simplest form in terms of composition, background and lighting. I am not always interested in trying to capture the true self of the sitter; often I project on to the subject my own preconceived idea of what I want the portrait to be. However, in the case of Andie, it was an honest attempt to convey her true self.'

INTERVIEW BY RICHARD MCCLURE

THE TAYLOR WESSING PHOTOGRAPHIC PORTRAIT PRIZE

EXHIBITORS

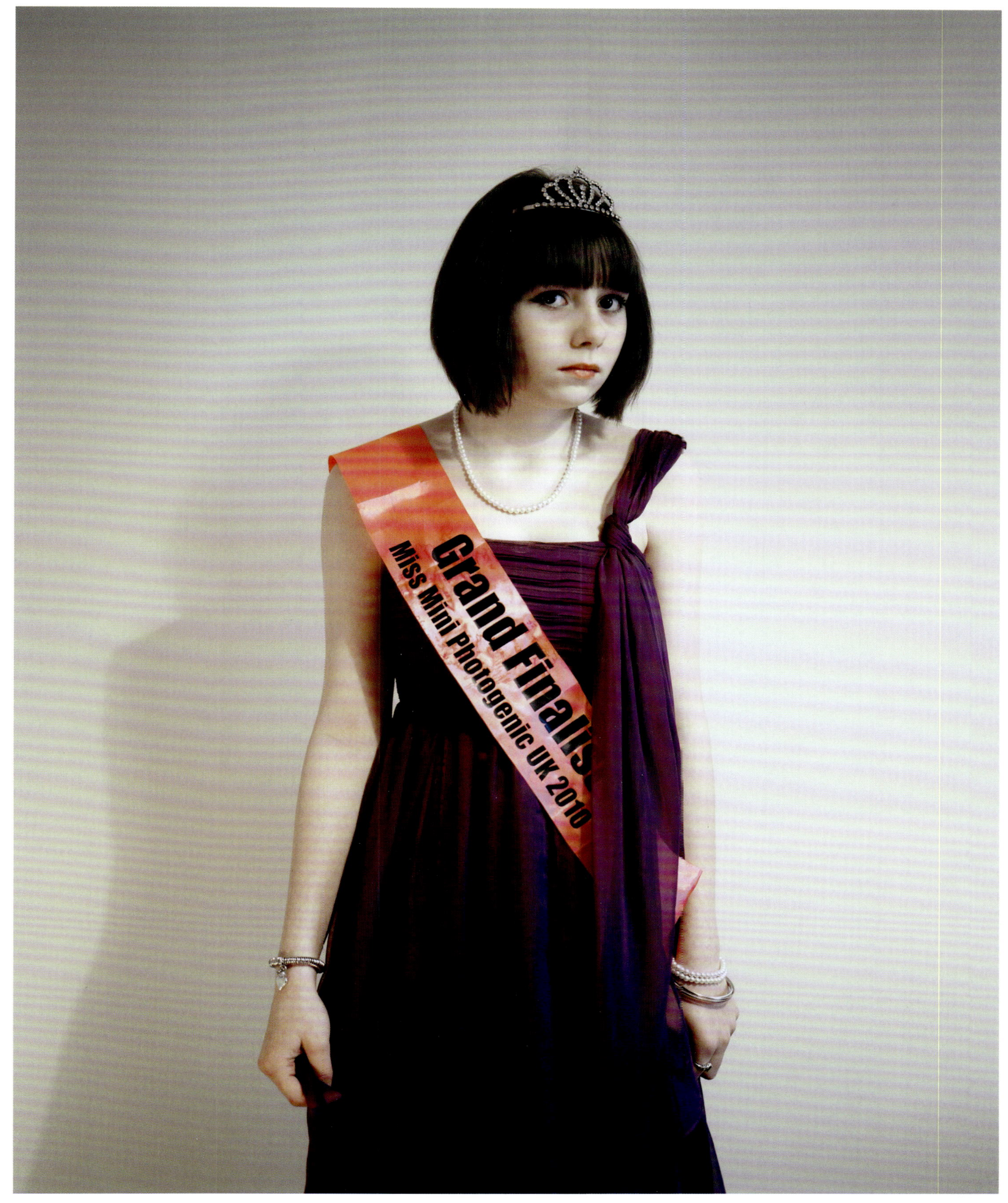

LIDIA KOWALEWICZ
MISS MINI PHOTOGENIC UK 2010
FROM THE SERIES *BEAUTY PAGEANTS*
JANUARY 2011

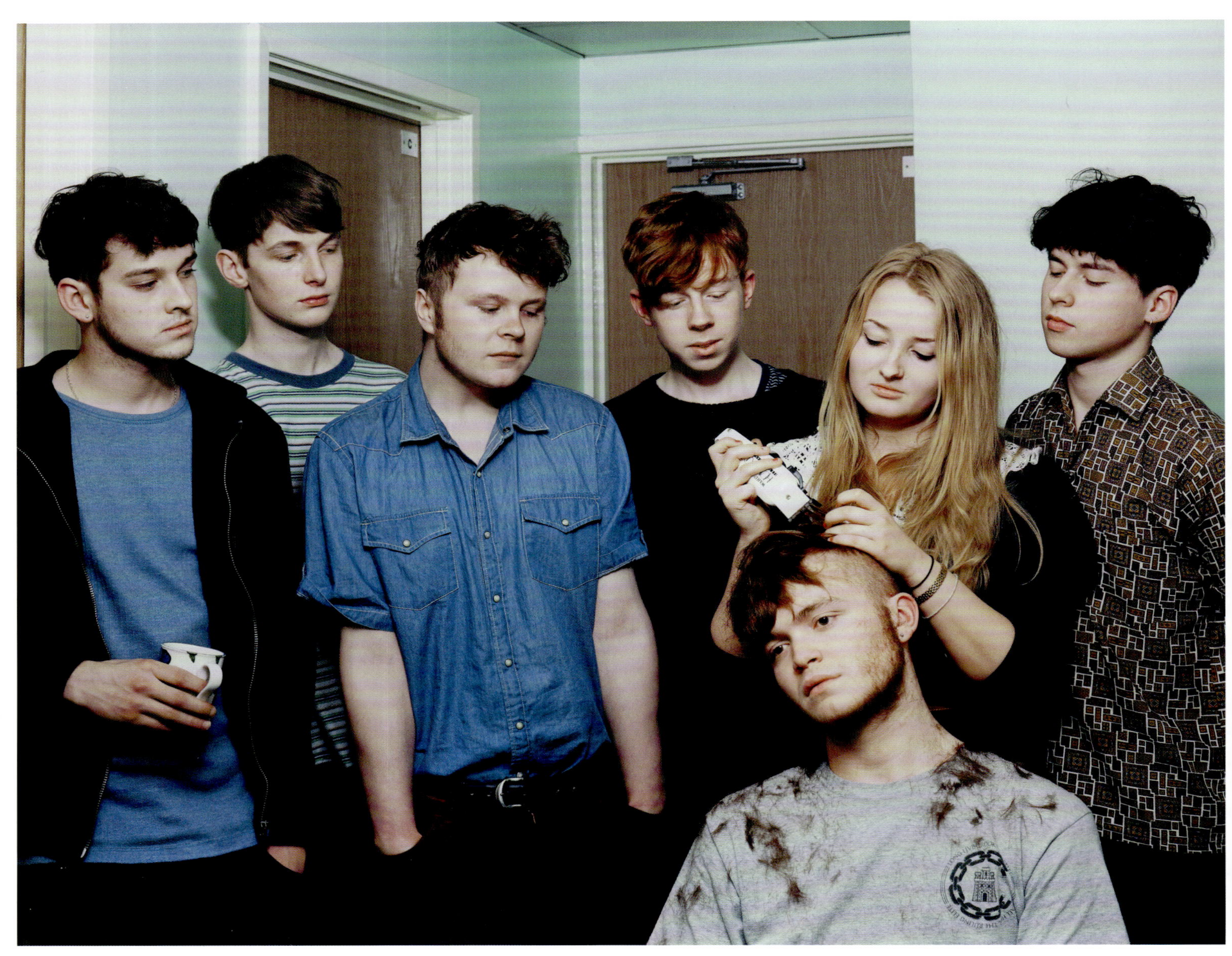

DAVID STEWART
THE SHEPHERDESS
FROM THE SERIES *TEENAGE PRE-OCCUPATION*
JANUARY 2011

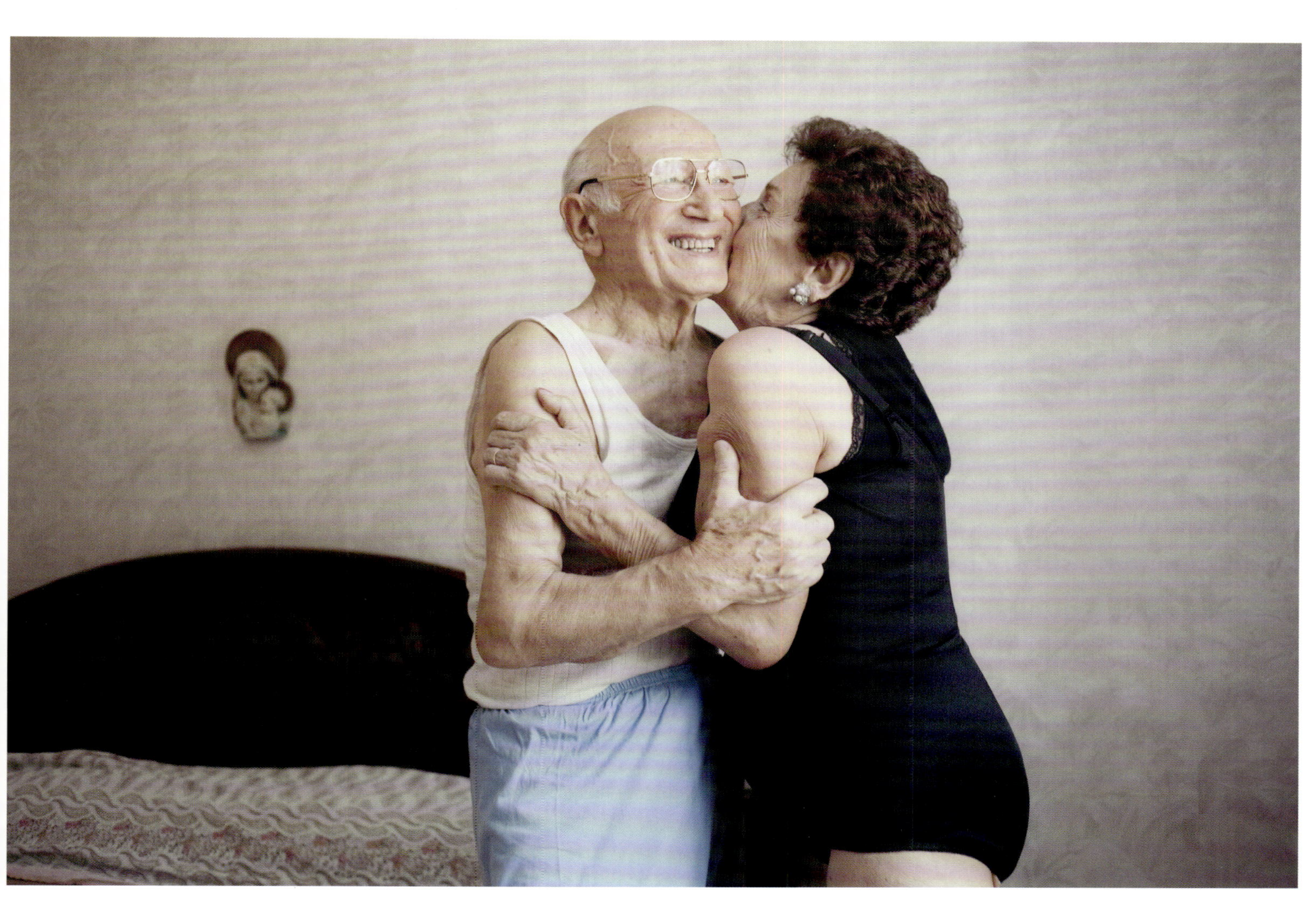

CLAUDIA BURLOTTI
ANNA AND ROBERTO AT HOME, ITALY #6153
FROM THE SERIES *EIGHTY FIVE*
AUGUST 2010

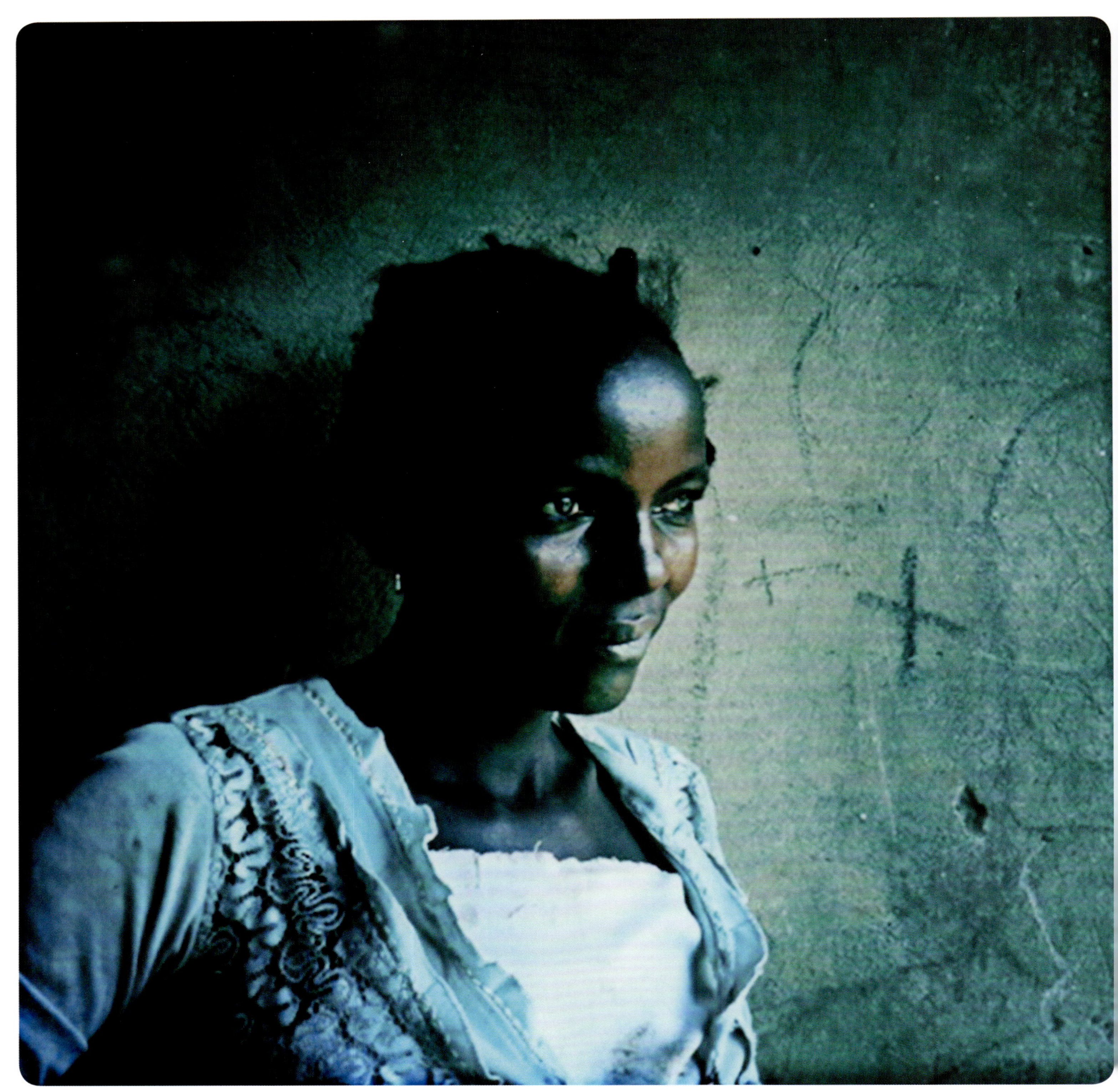

CAROL ALLEN STOREY
GRACE
FROM THE SERIES *'RELUCTANT' SEX WORKERS*
JUNE 2011

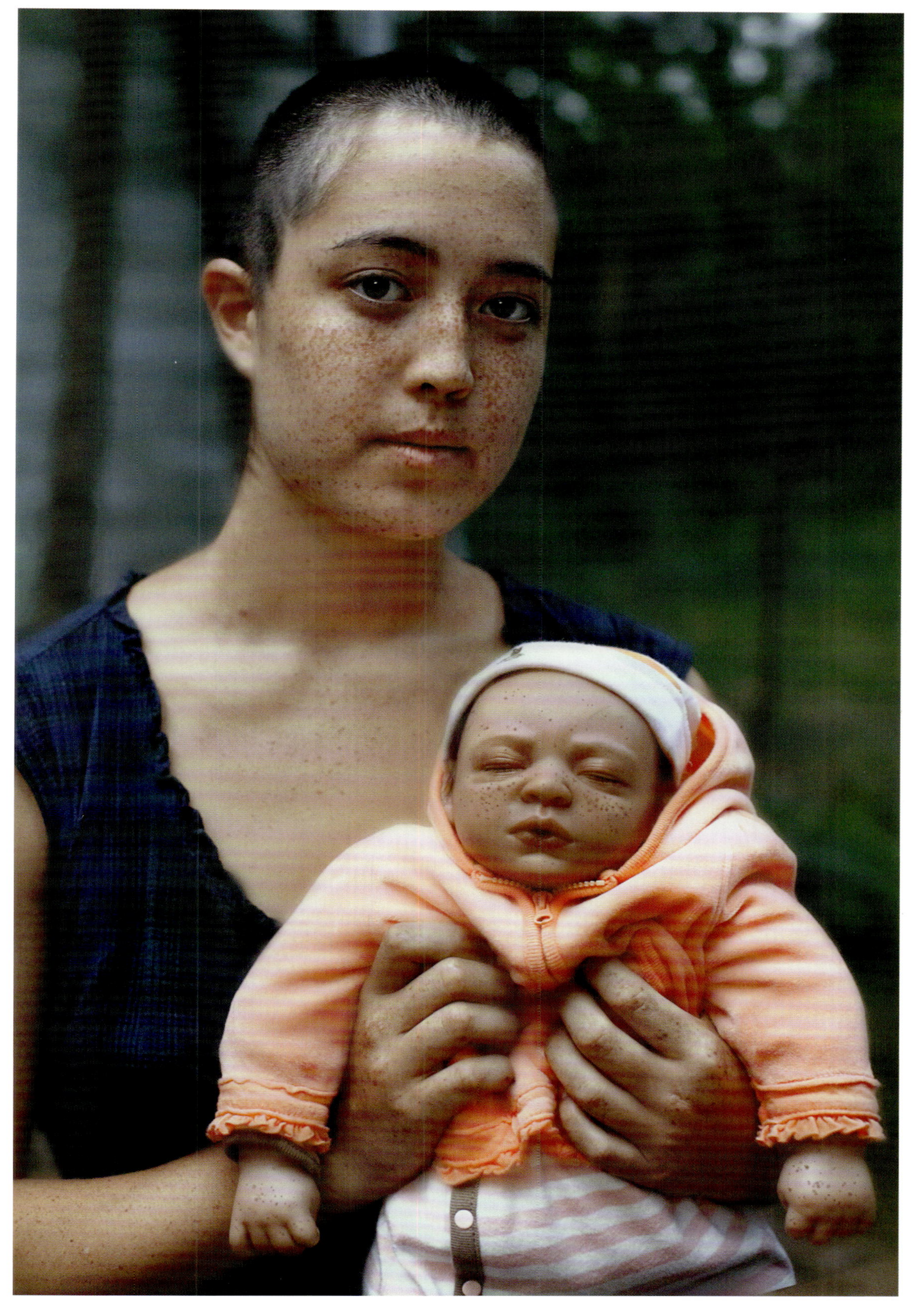

REBECCA MARTINEZ
ZOILA WITH FRECKLES
FROM THE SERIES *PRETENDERS*
JUNE 2010

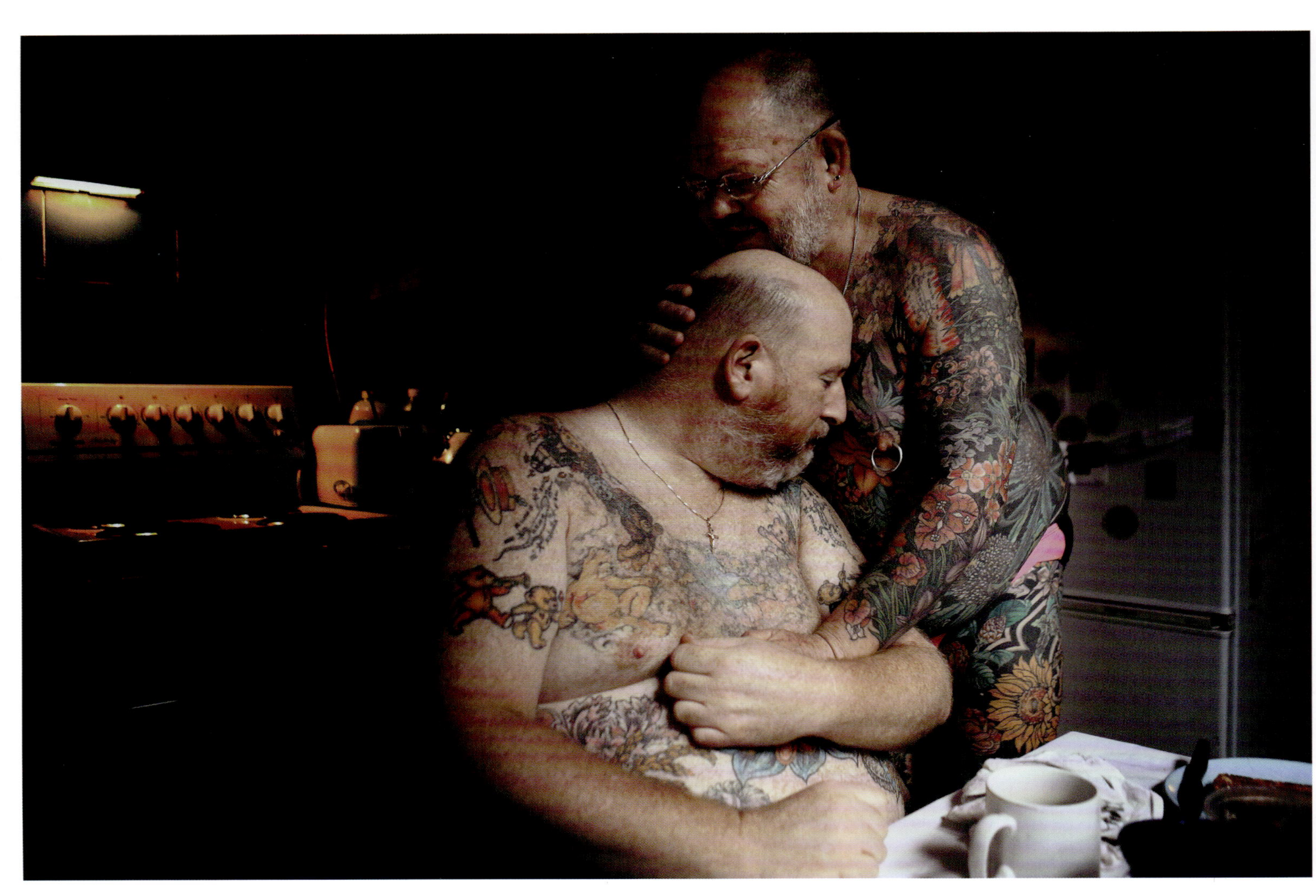

JONATHAN MAY
THE EMBRACE
FROM THE SERIES *HOT INK*
FEBRUARY 2010

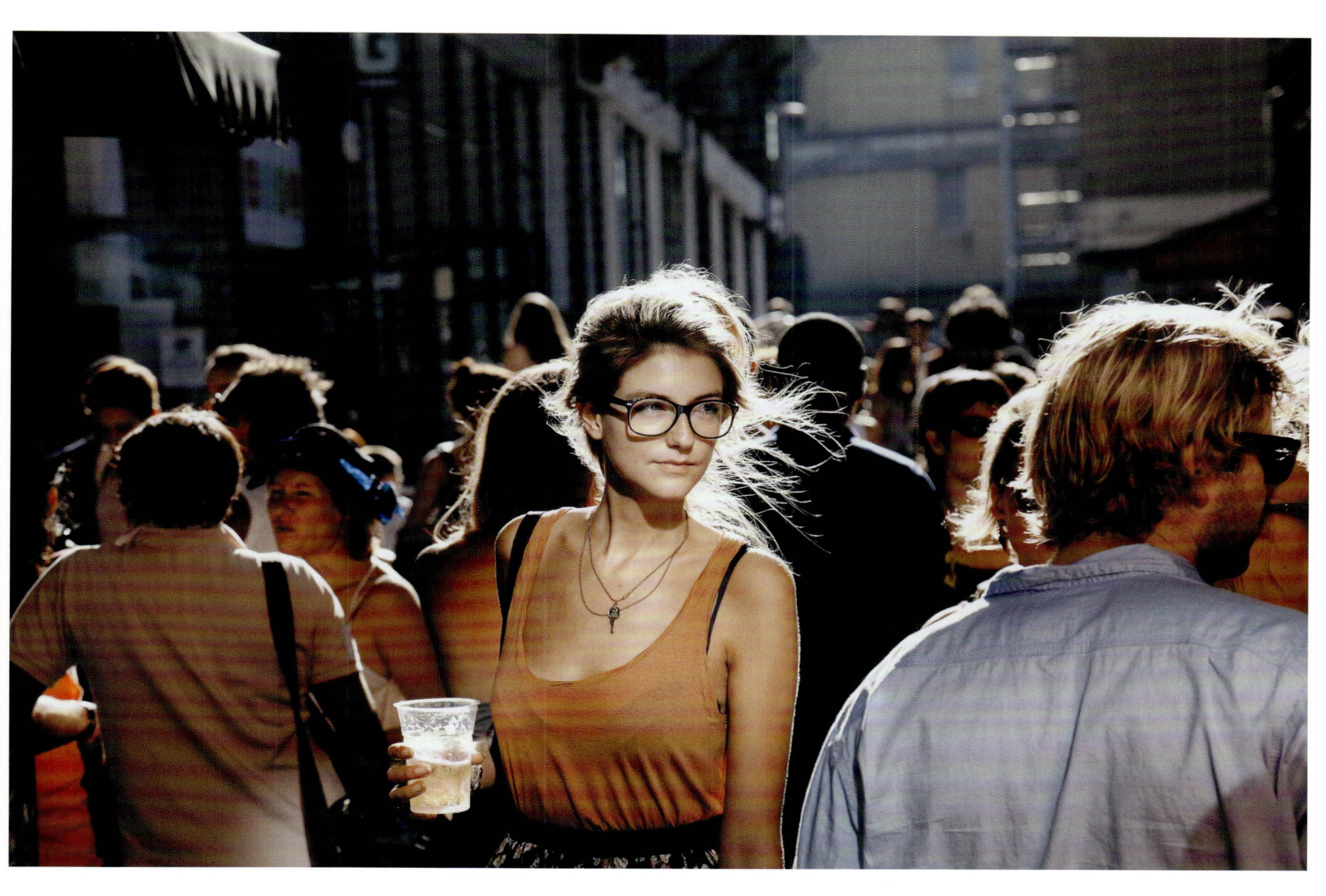

DARREN HALL
OLD TRUMAN BREWERY/CLAUDIA
JUNE 2011

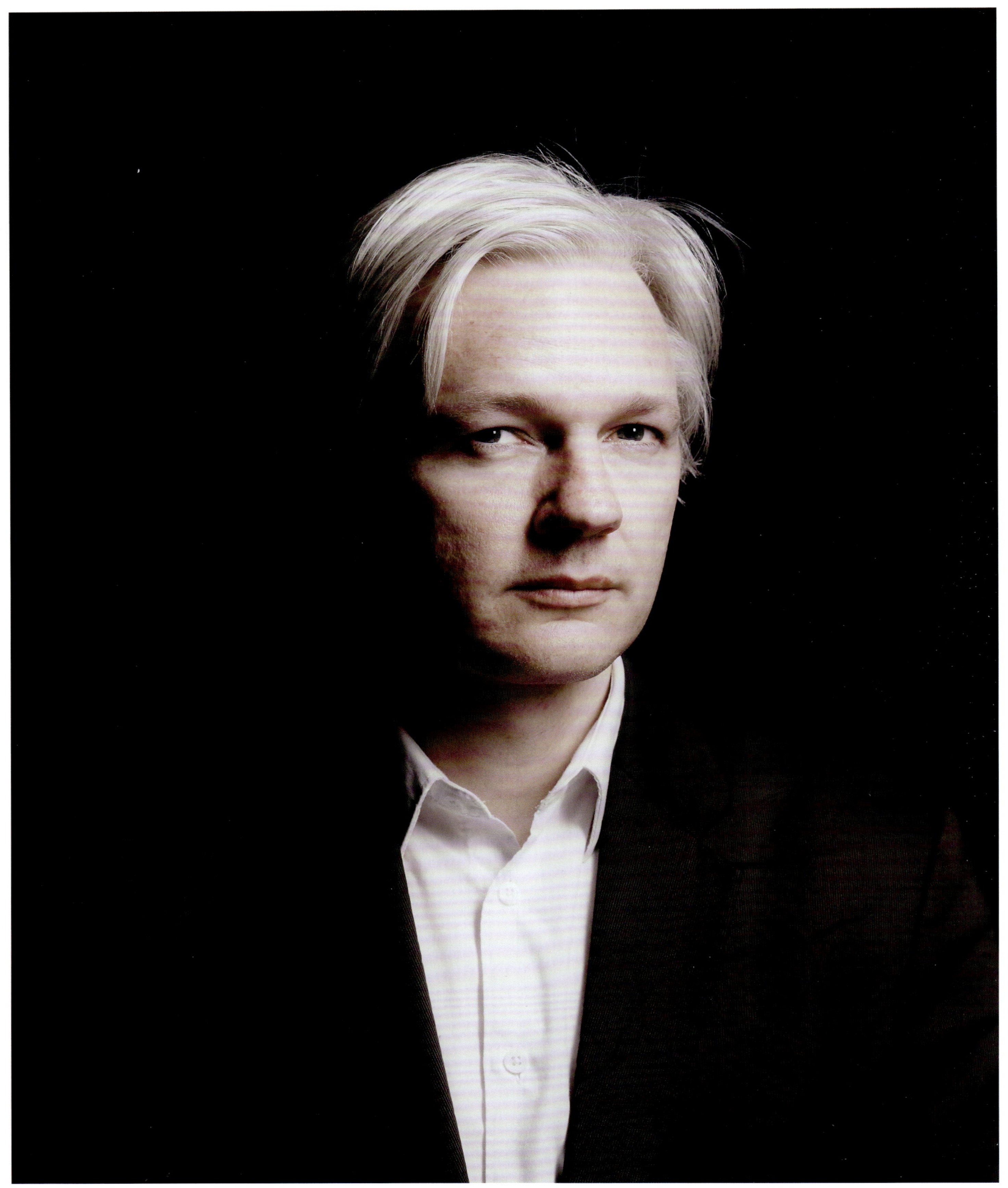

KATE PETERS
JULIAN ASSANGE, FOUNDER OF WIKILEAKS
JULY 2010

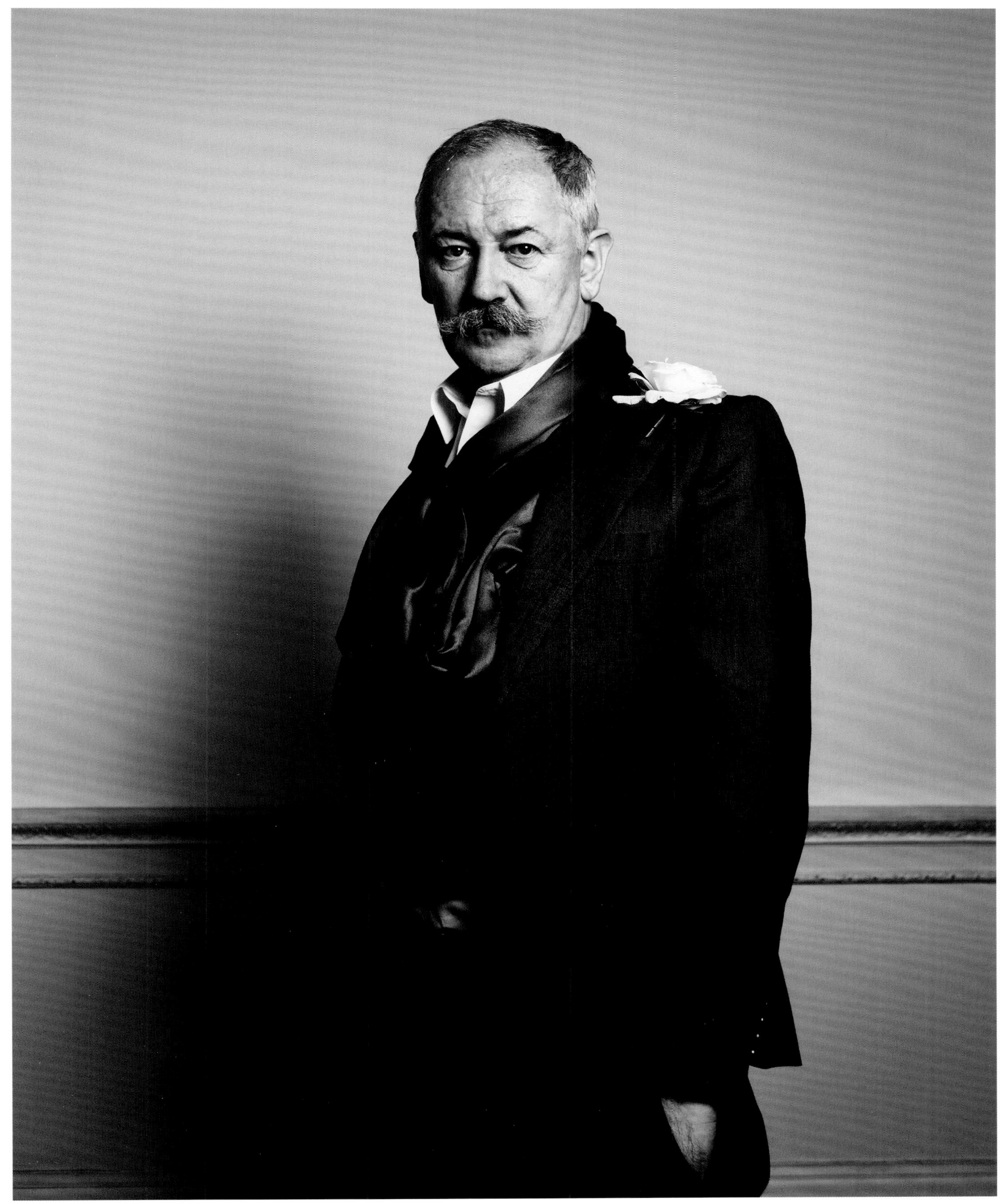

MARK BLOWER
CERITH WYN EVANS
FROM THE SERIES *ARTISTS*
OCTOBER 2010

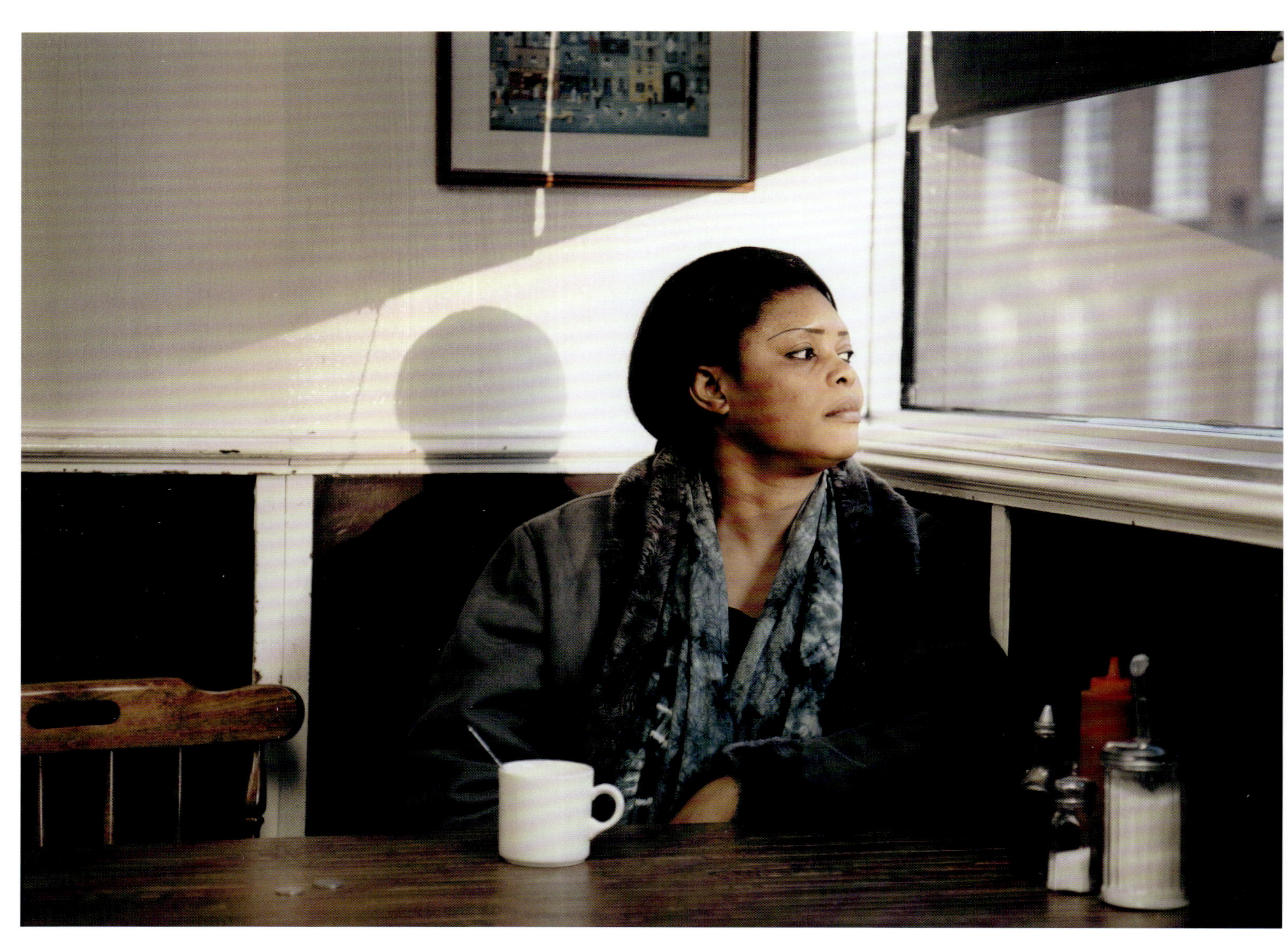

SIMON BREMNER
TERRY
NOVEMBER 2010

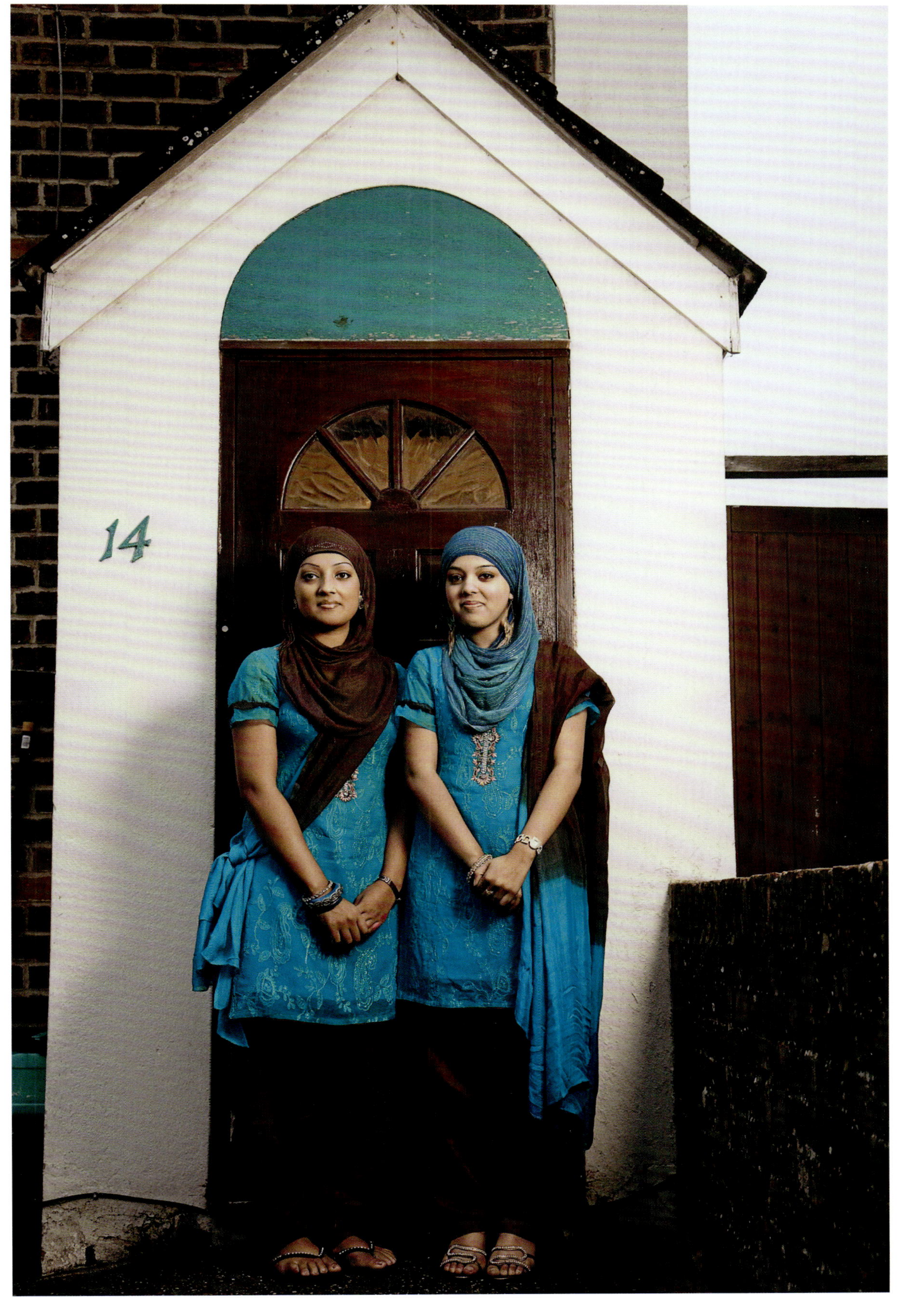

LAURA HASKELL
ROWSONARA & ZARA
FROM THE SERIES *THE BANGLADESHI COMMUNITY PORTRAITS*
NOVEMBER 2010

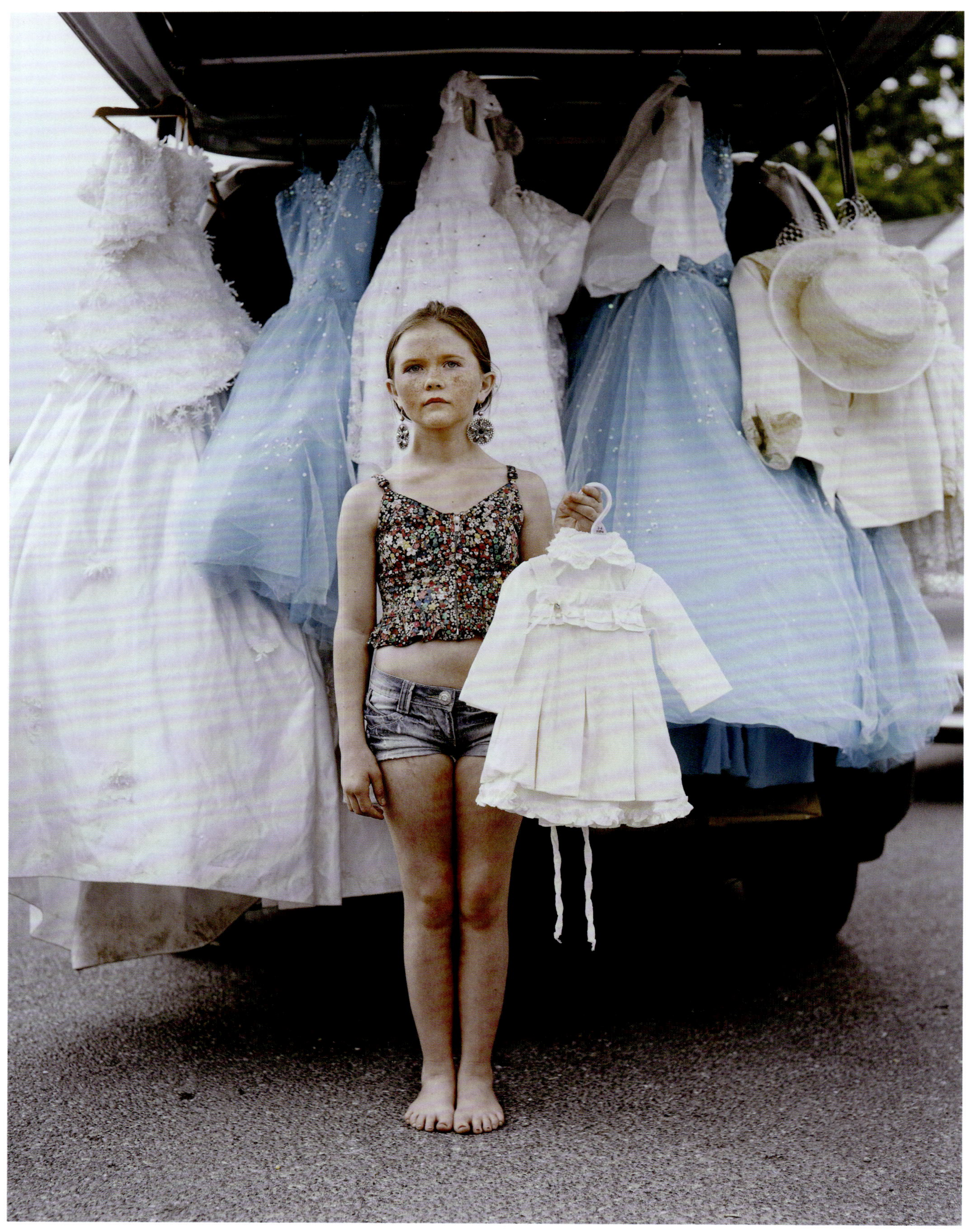

KENNETH O HALLORAN
OLIVE SELLING DRESSES
SEPTEMBER 2010

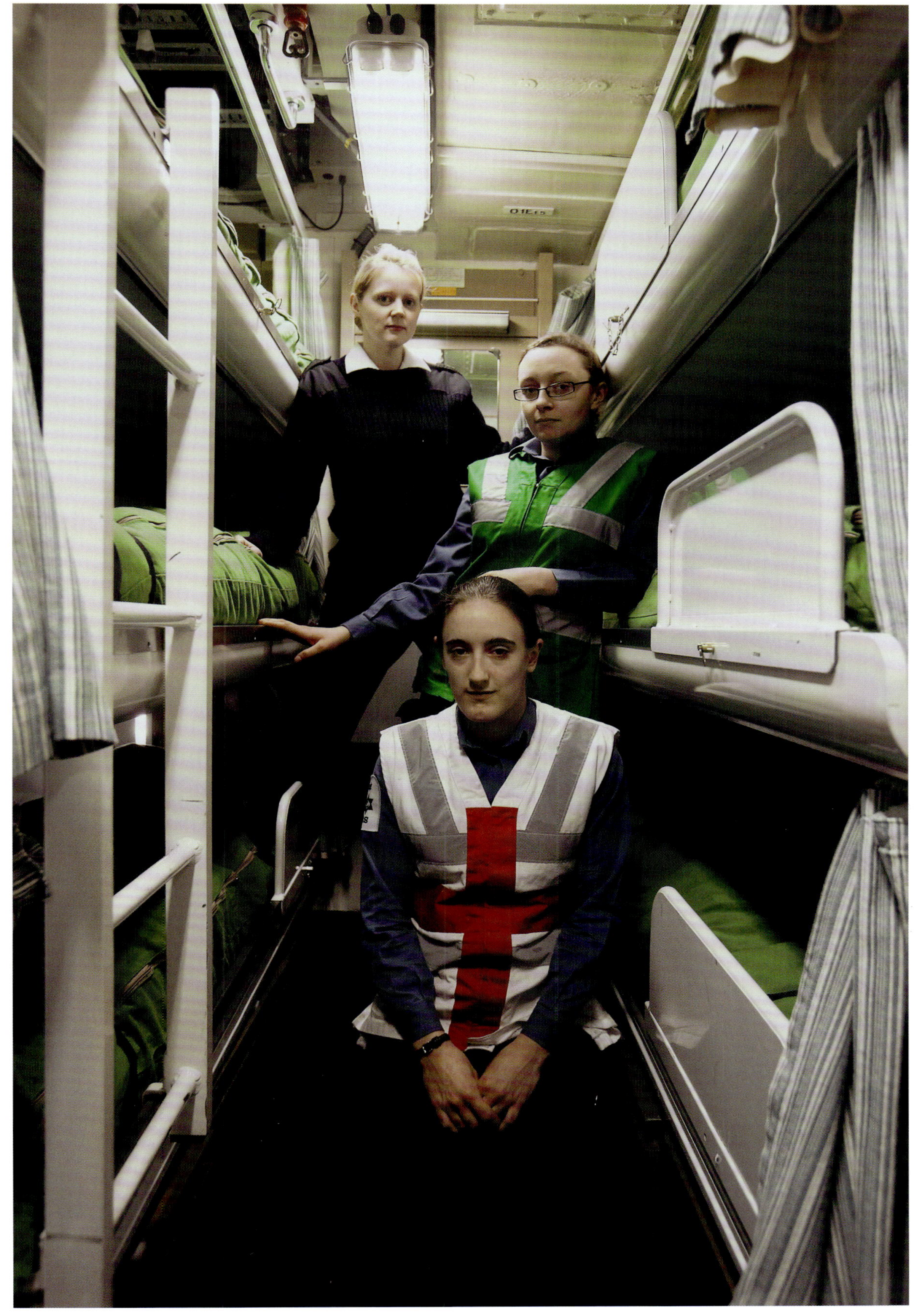

ADRIAN PEACOCK
WRENS QUARTERS
FROM THE SERIES *HMS BULWARK*
MARCH 2011

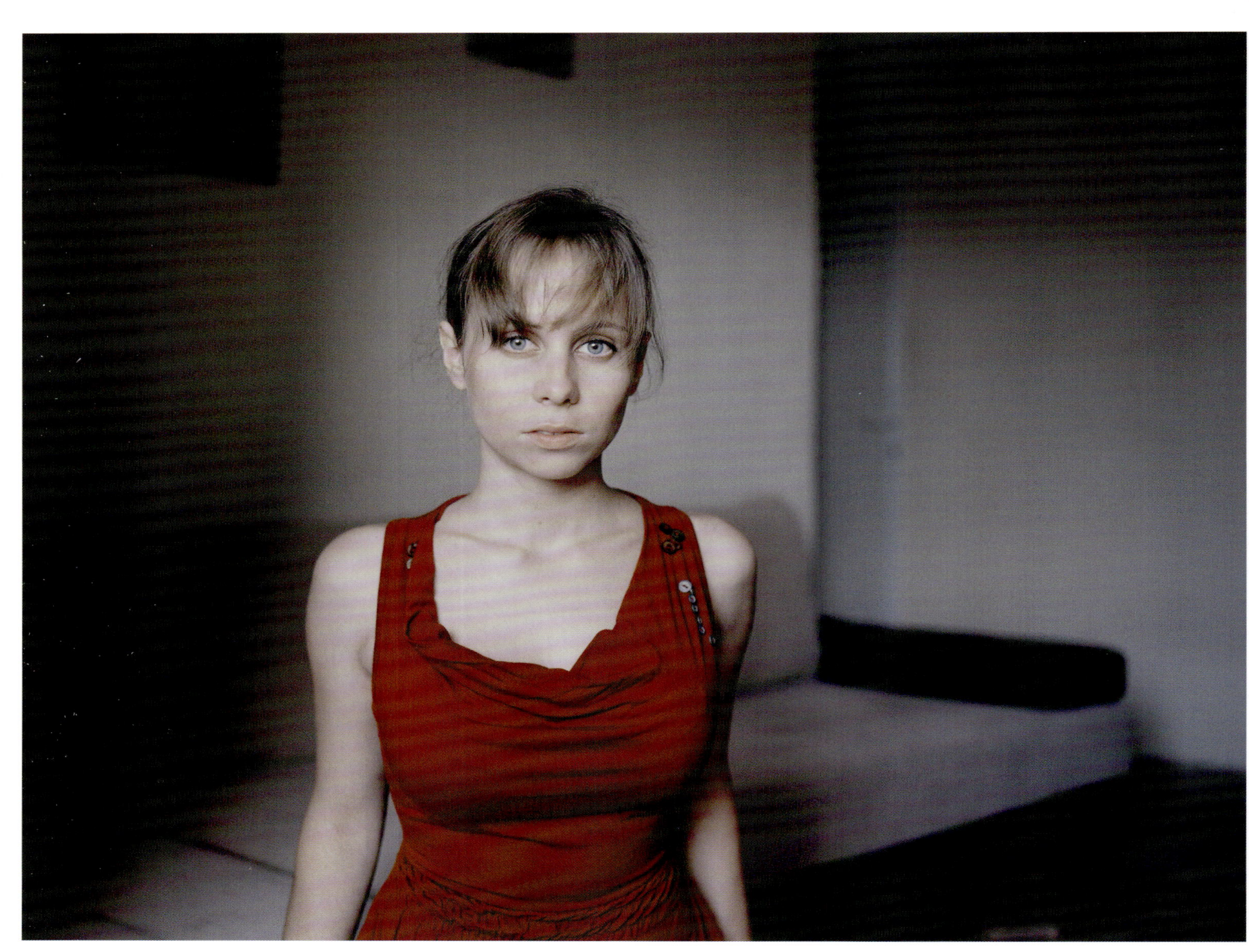

HADAS MUALEM
SVETA
MAY 2011

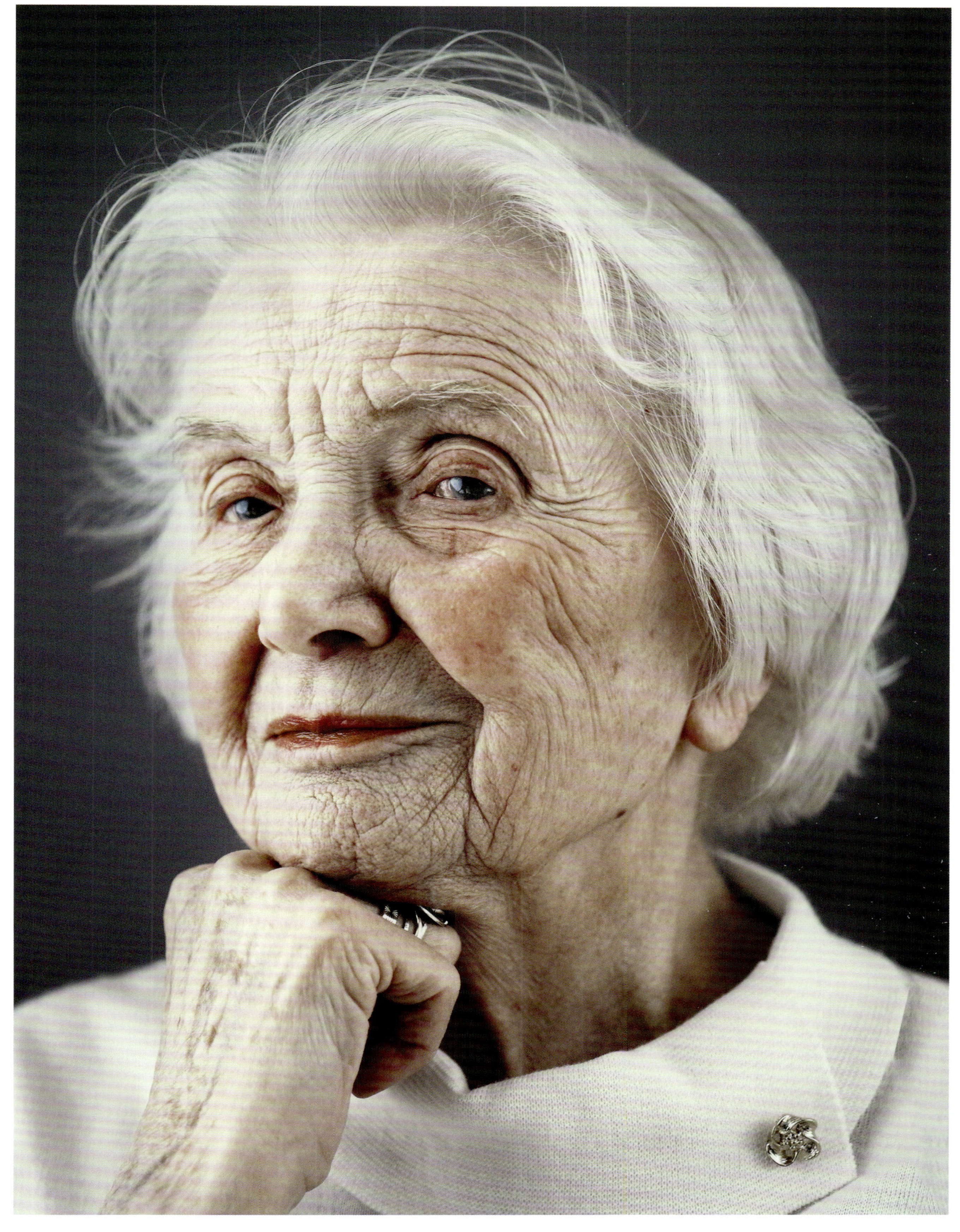

KARSTEN THORMAEHLEN
ERIKA E., BORN IN 1910
FROM THE SERIES *HAPPY AT ONE HUNDRED*
MARCH 2011

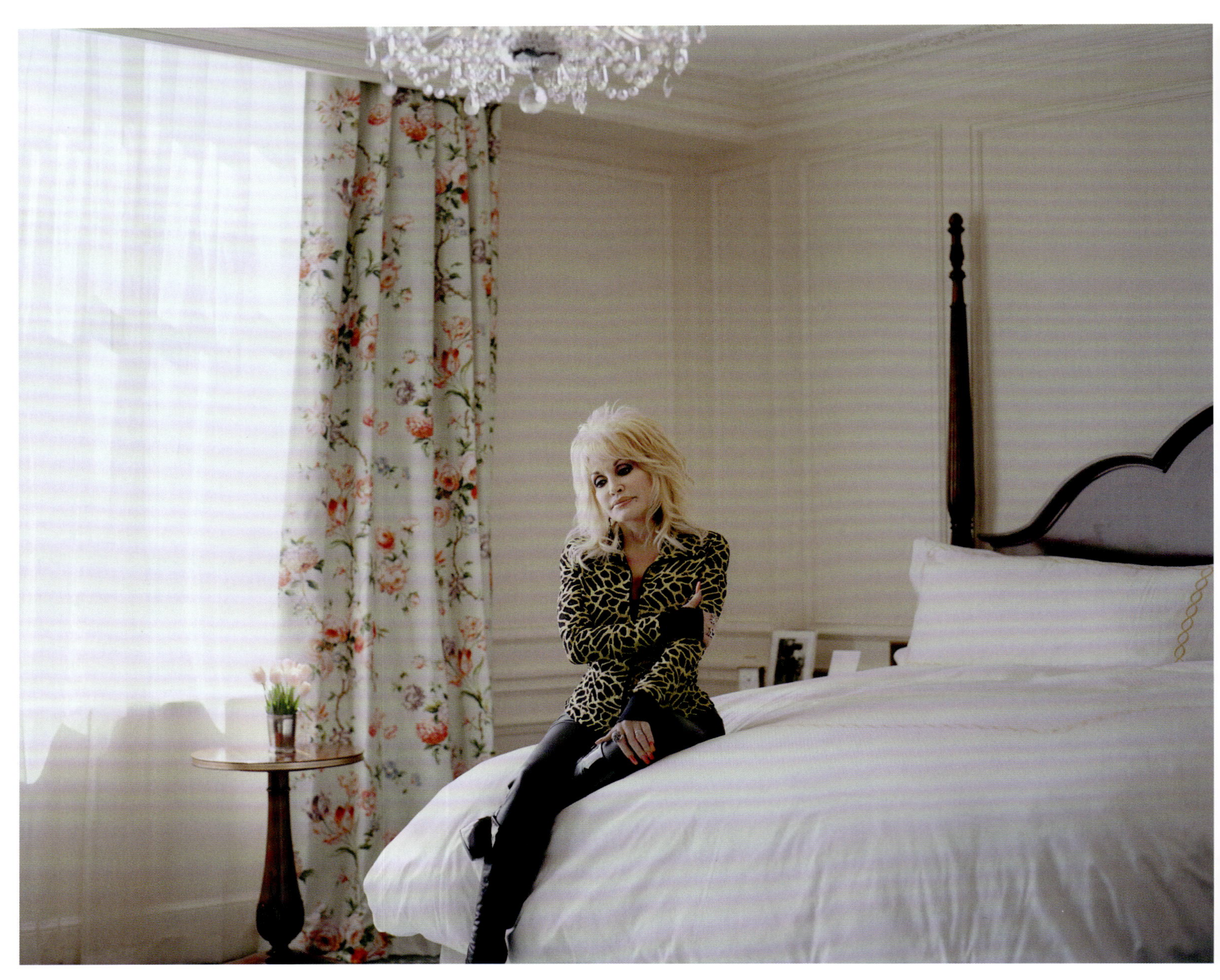

ZED NELSON
DOLLY PARTON
APRIL 2011

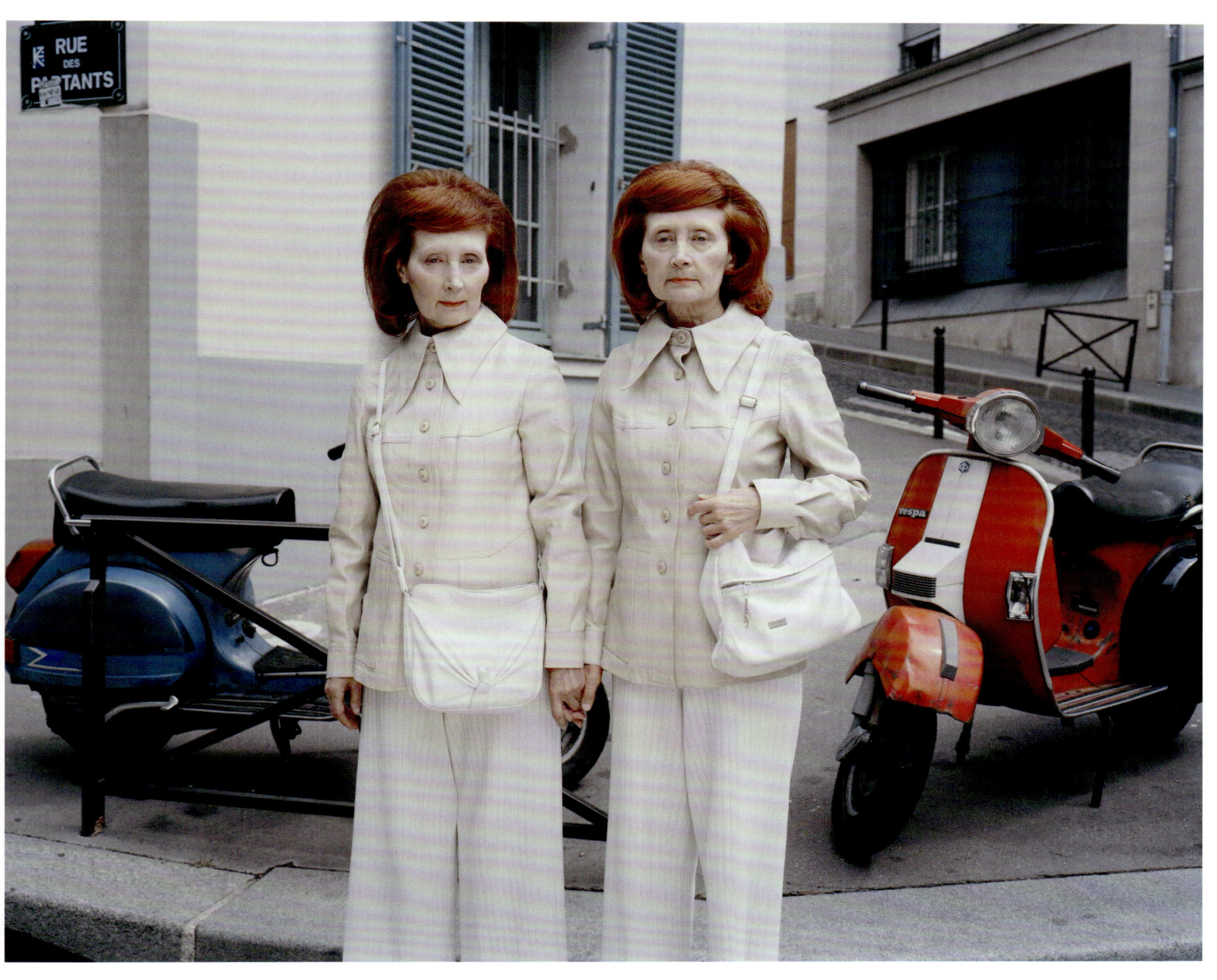

MAJA DANIELS
MONETTE AND MADY, RUE DES PARTANTS
JULY 2010

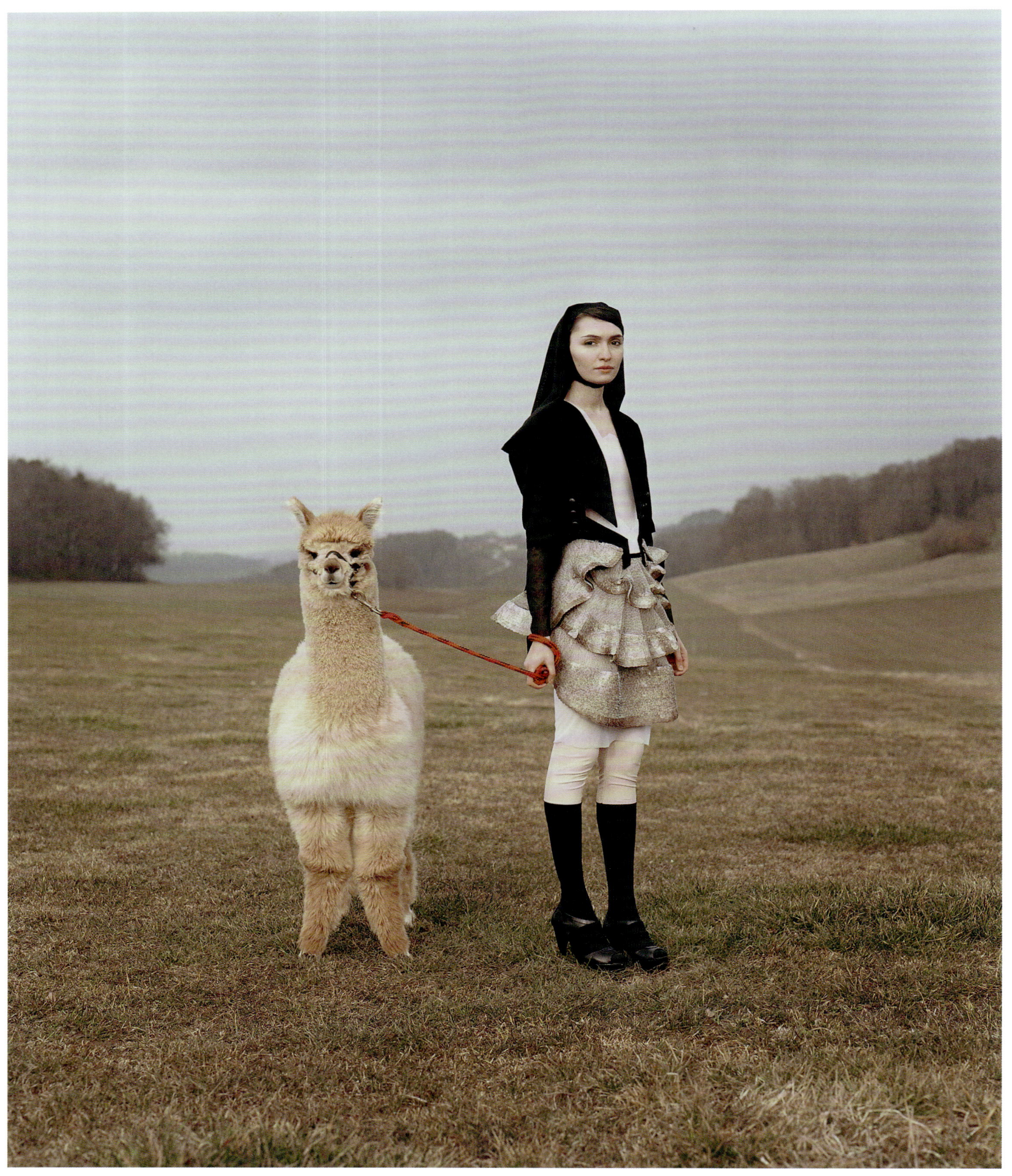

YANN GROSS
TATIANA AND BELENE
FROM THE SERIES *VENUS & FURS*
FEBRUARY 2011

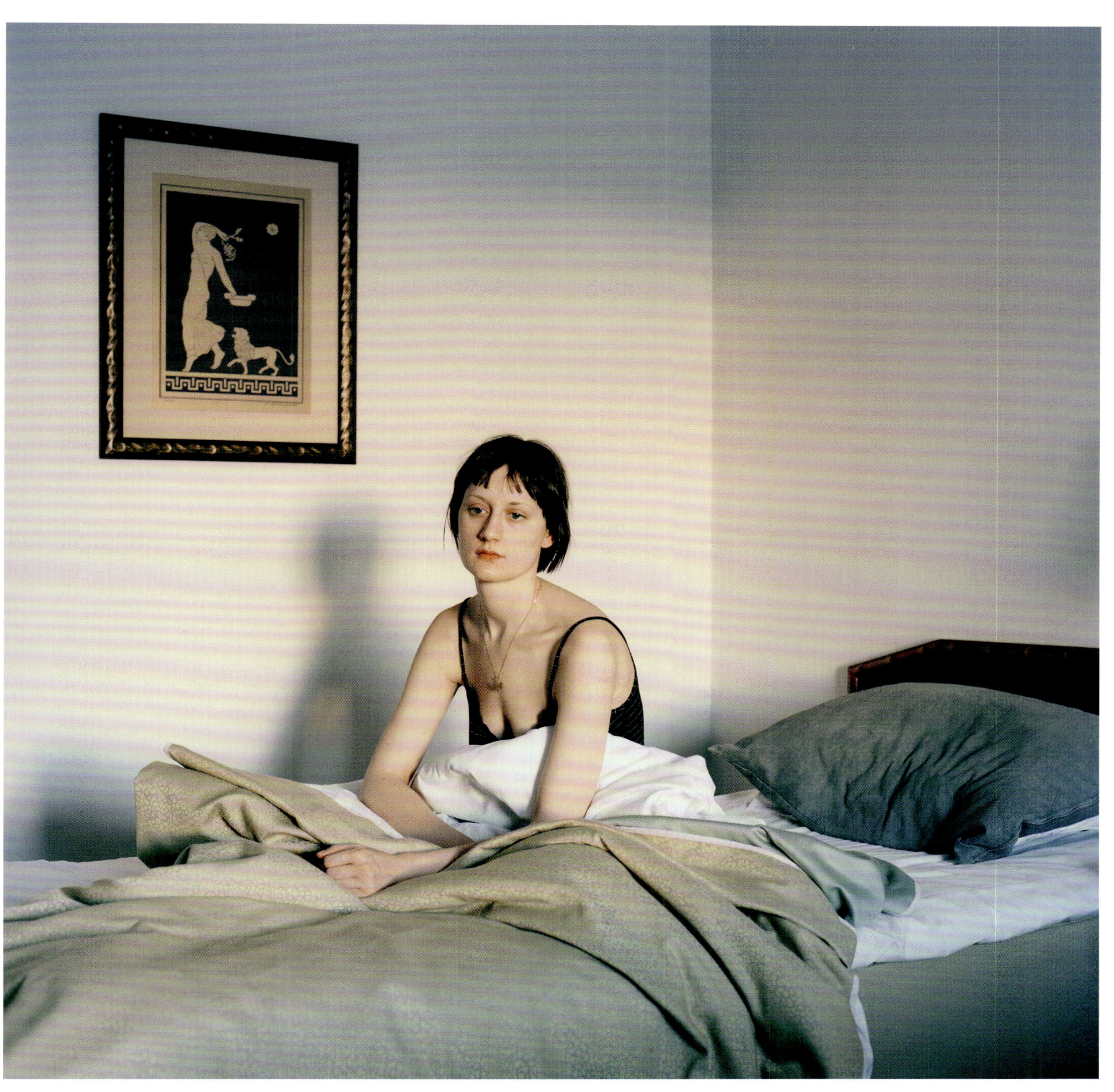

TINA HILLIER
MELINDA, FINLAND
JANUARY 2011

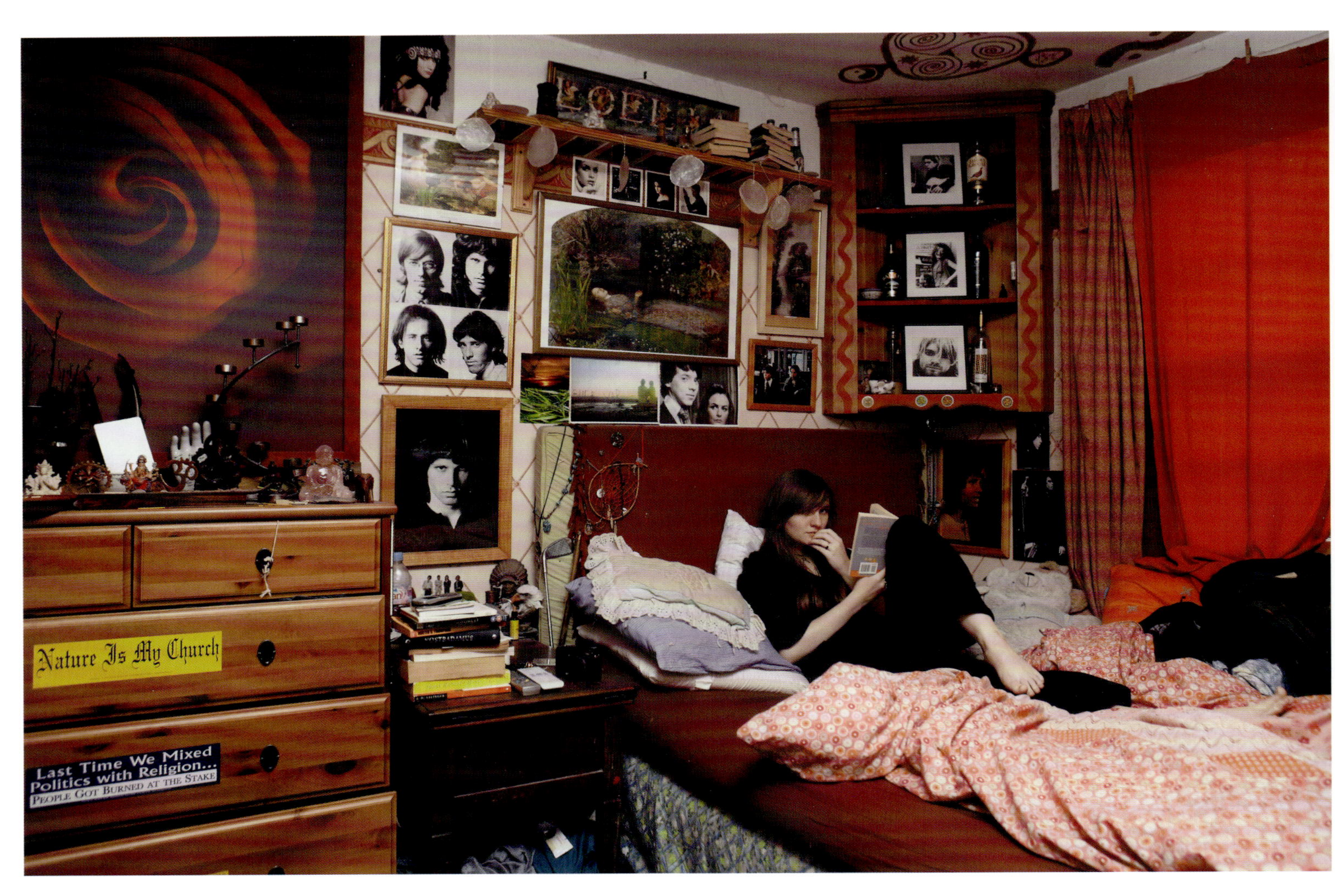

ARAMINTA DE CLERMONT

LOELIA

FROM THE SERIES *A SPACE OF MY OWN*

OCTOBER 2010

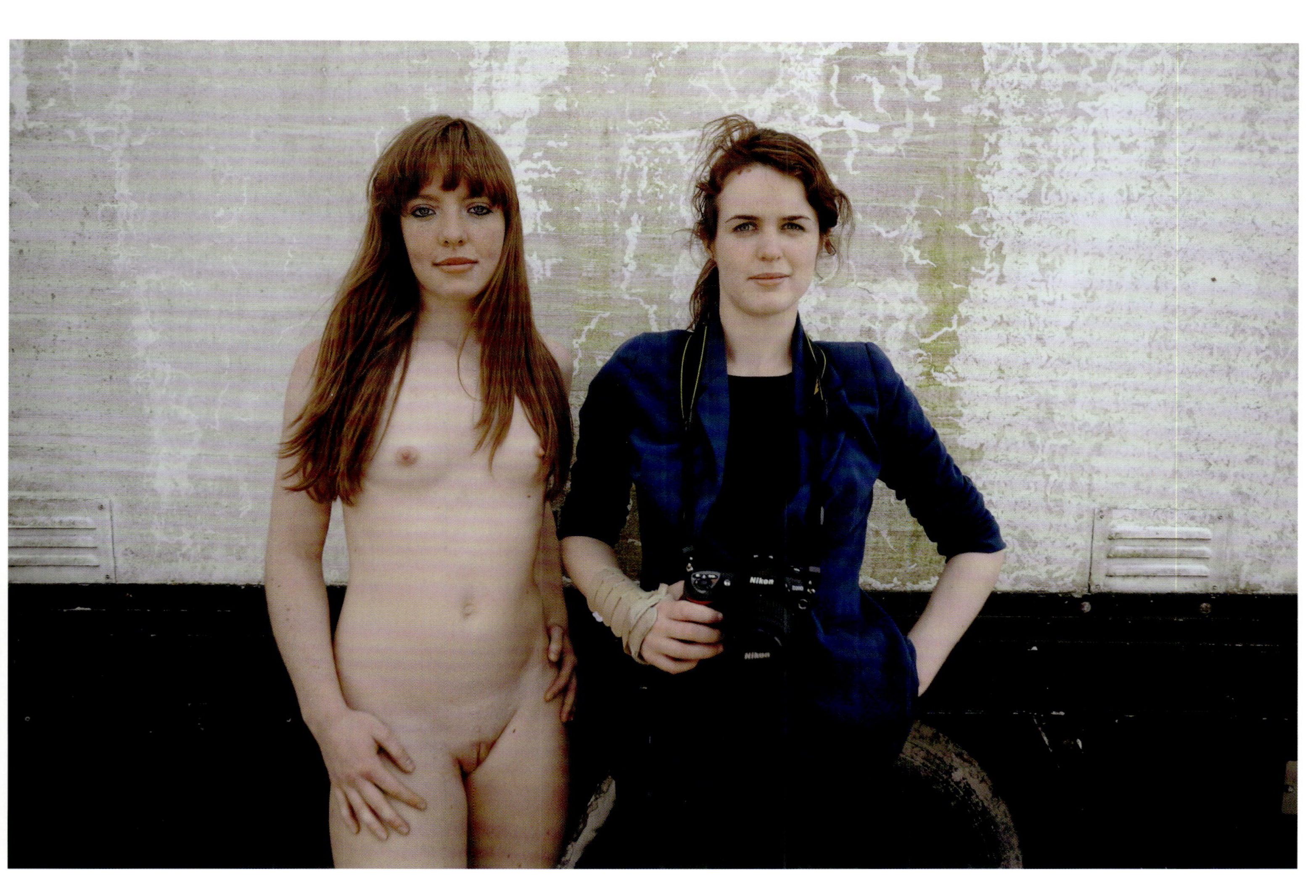

COLIN HAMPDEN-WHITE

NORMIO AND MISS HK

FROM THE SERIES *BRIGHTON GROUP SHOOT*

JUNE 2010

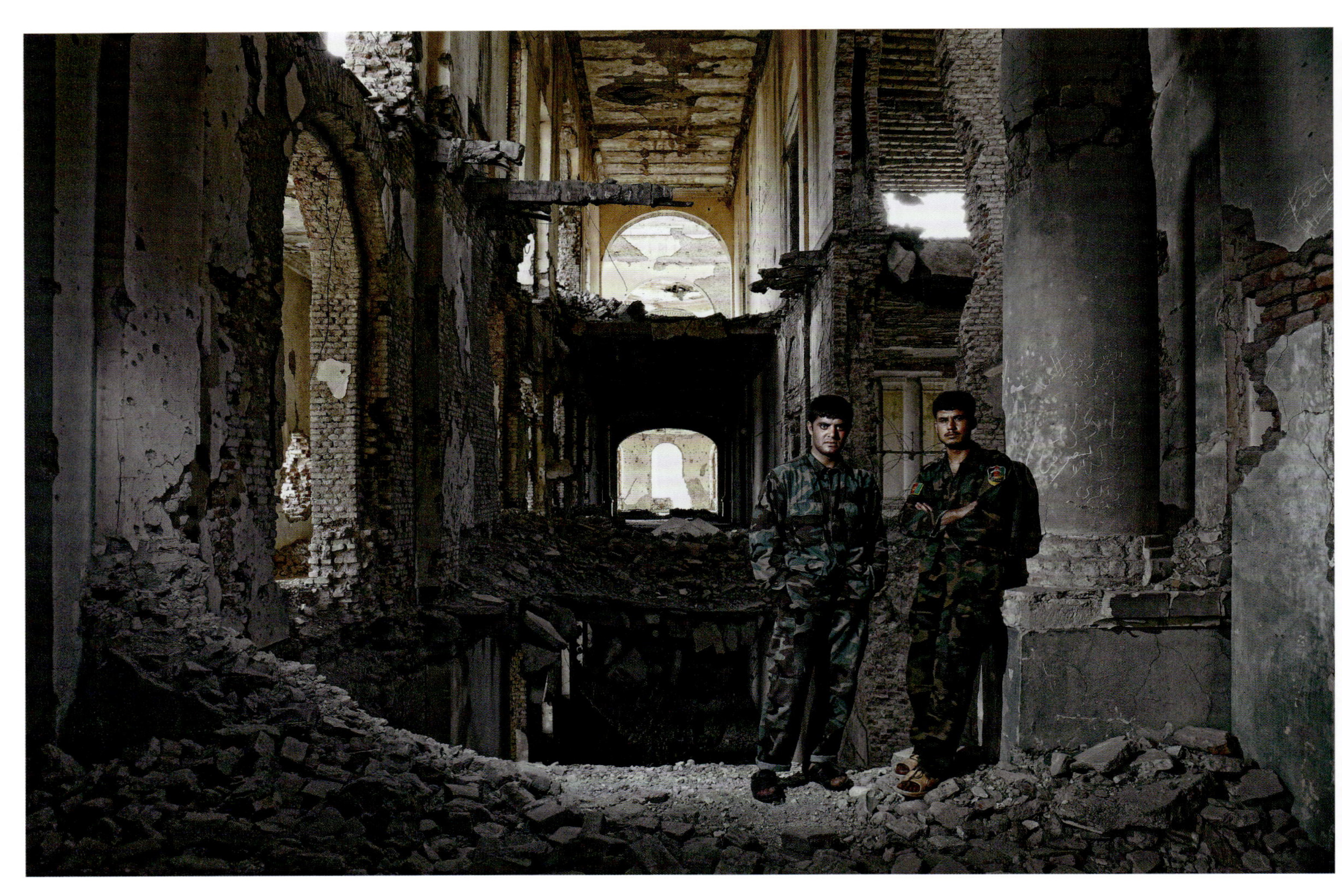

JEREMY RATA
THE KING'S PALACE KABUL
FROM THE SERIES AND BOOK *AFGHAN FACES – A SERIES OF PORTRAITS OF ORDINARY PEOPLE AFFECTED BY LIVING IN AFGHANISTAN*
AUGUST 2010

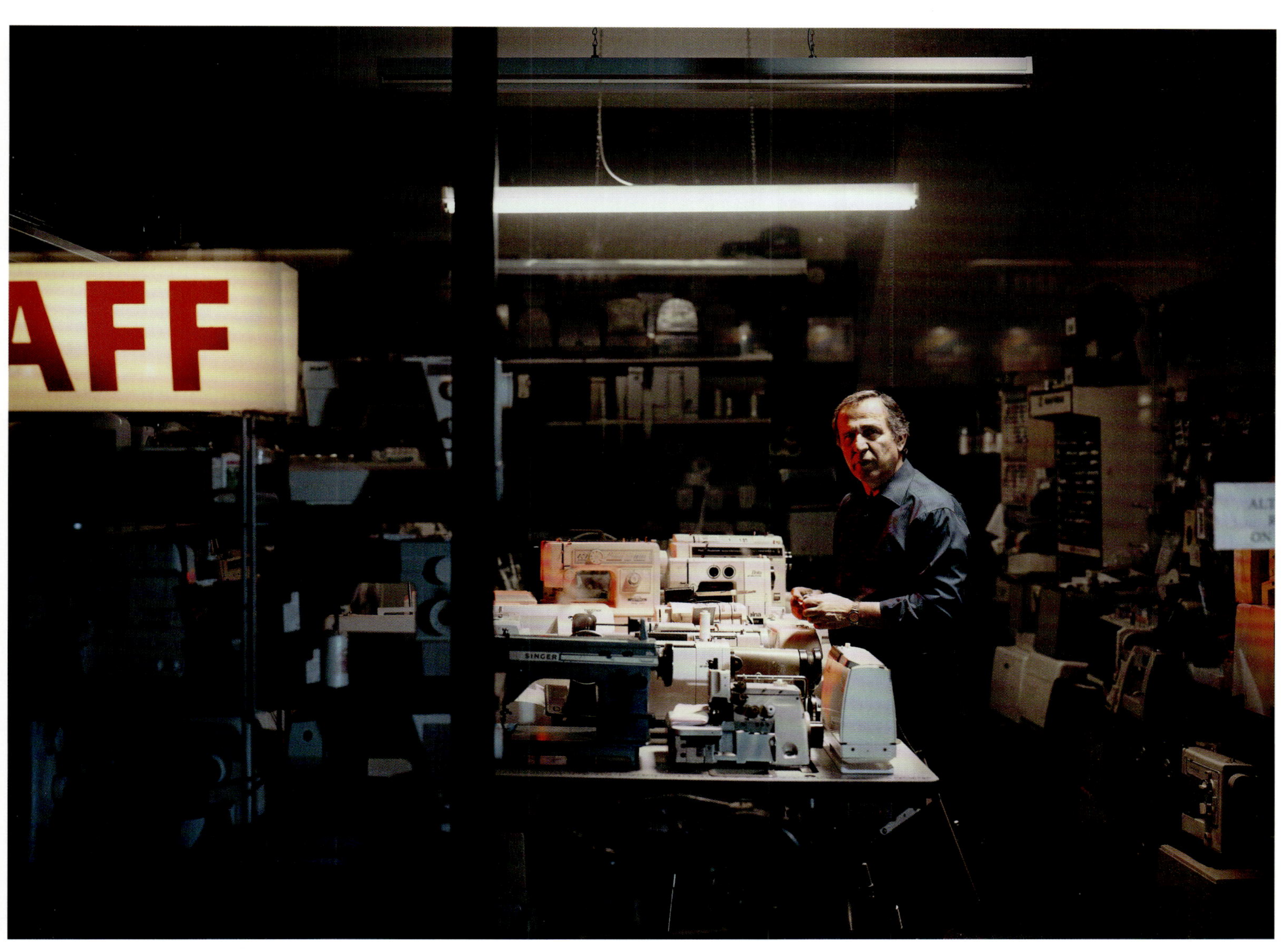

DYLAN COLLARD
TONY
FROM THE SERIES *UP MY STREET*
MARCH 2011

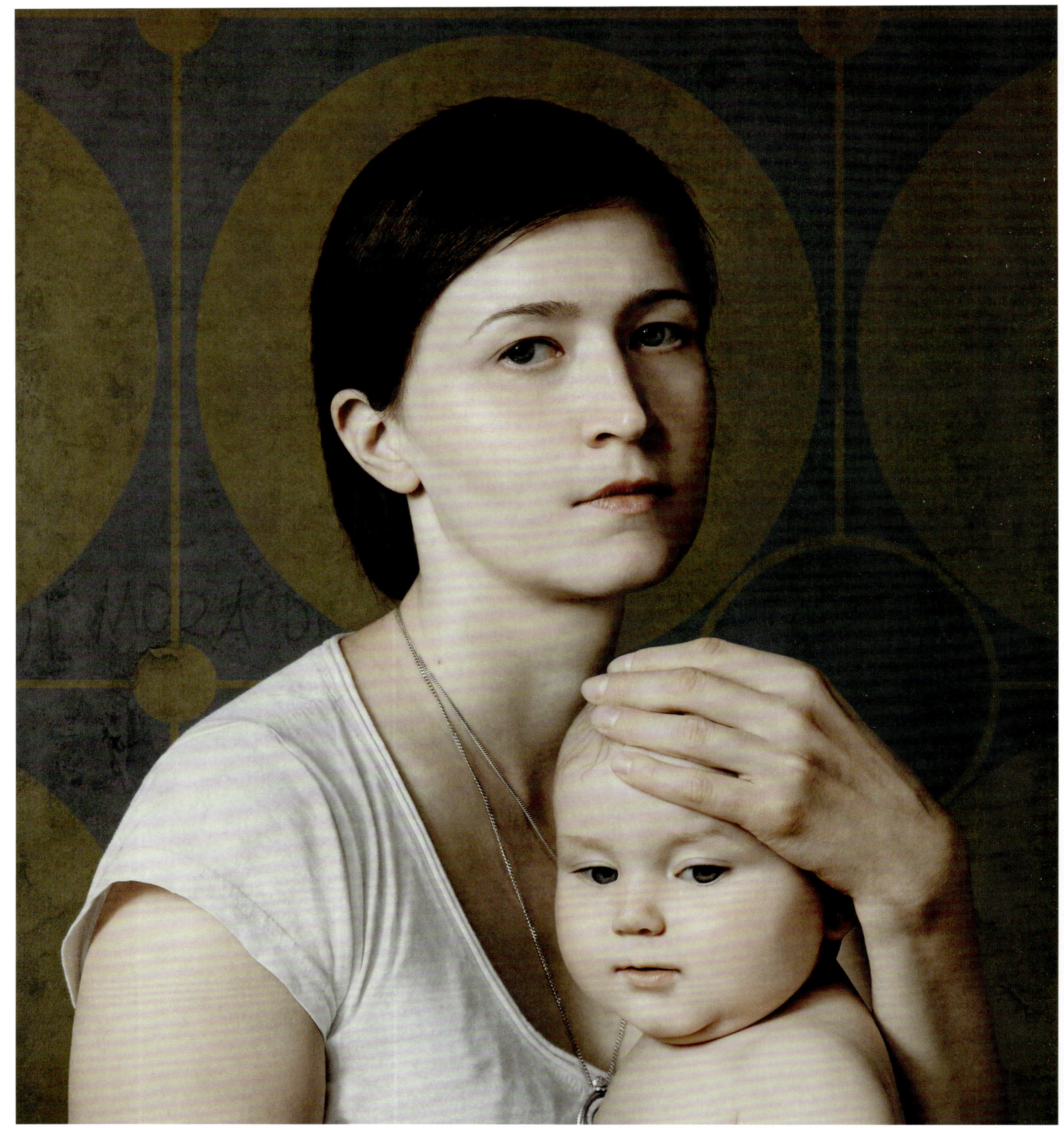

JULIA SCHESTAG
ELENA
FROM THE SERIES *ABOUT RESPONSIBILITY. PART 1. MARY*
APRIL 2011

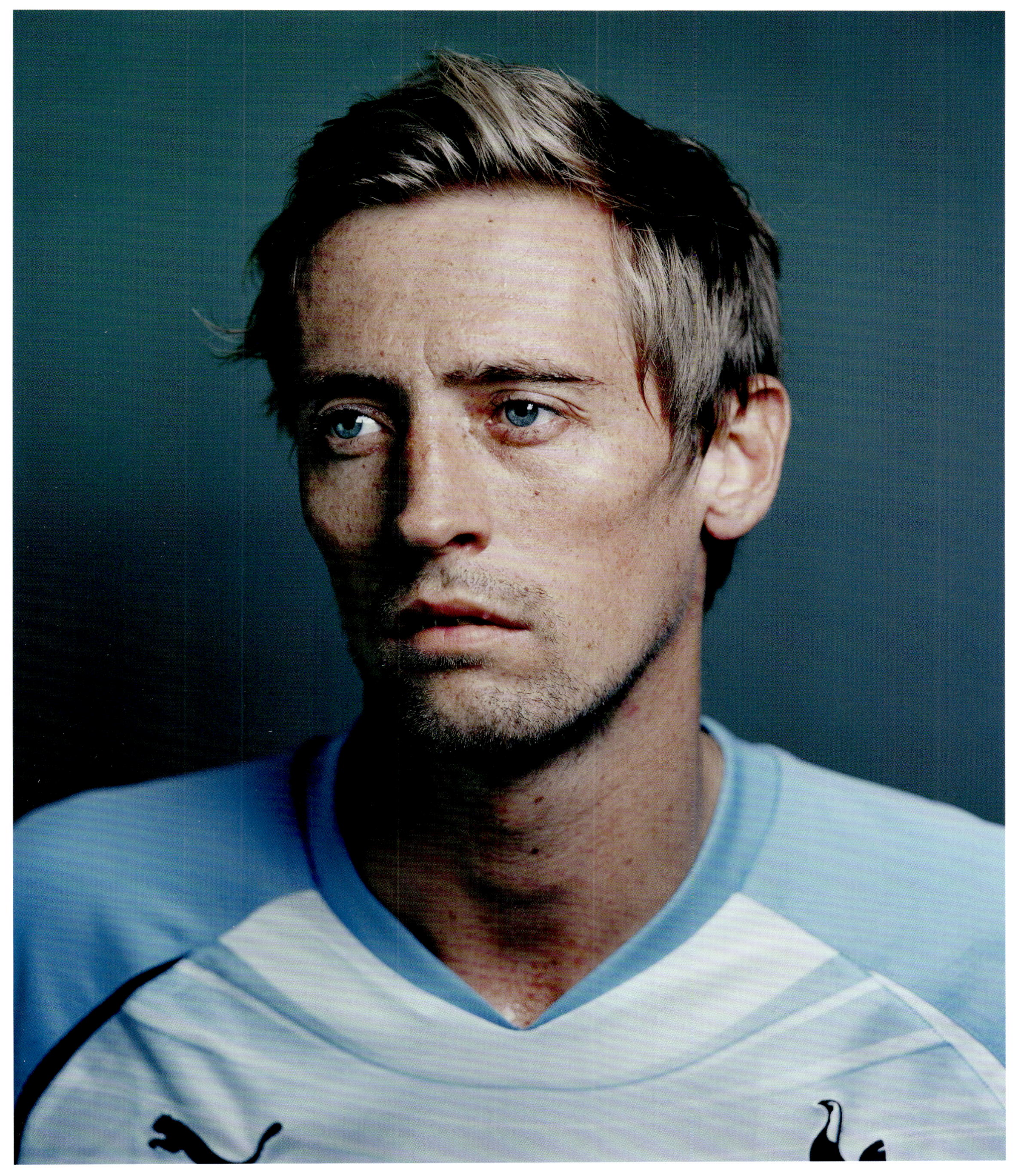

SPENCER MURPHY
PETER CROUCH
AUGUST 2010

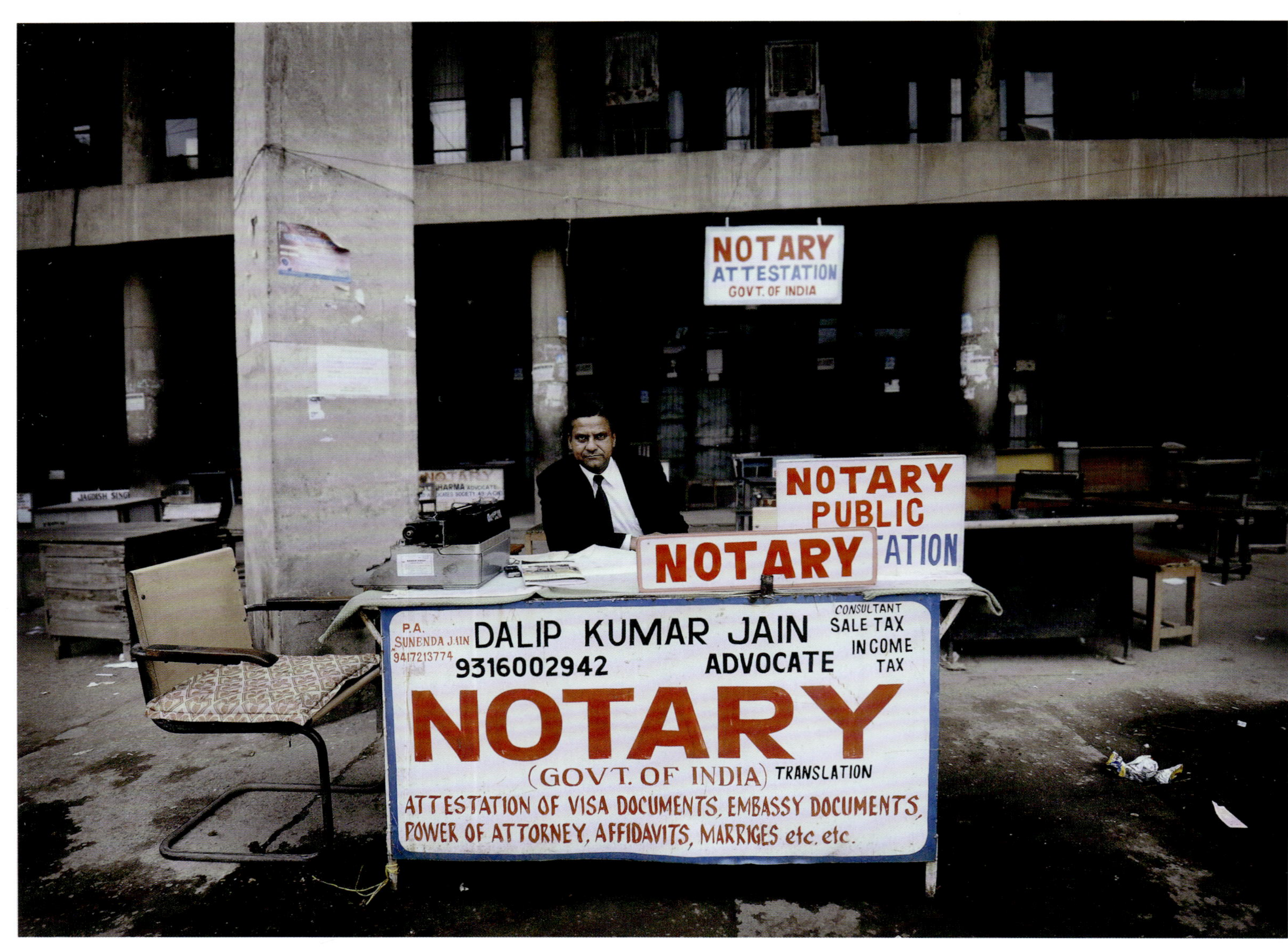

OLAF BALLNUS
DR. KUMAR
FROM THE SERIES *CHANDIGARH*
MARCH 2011

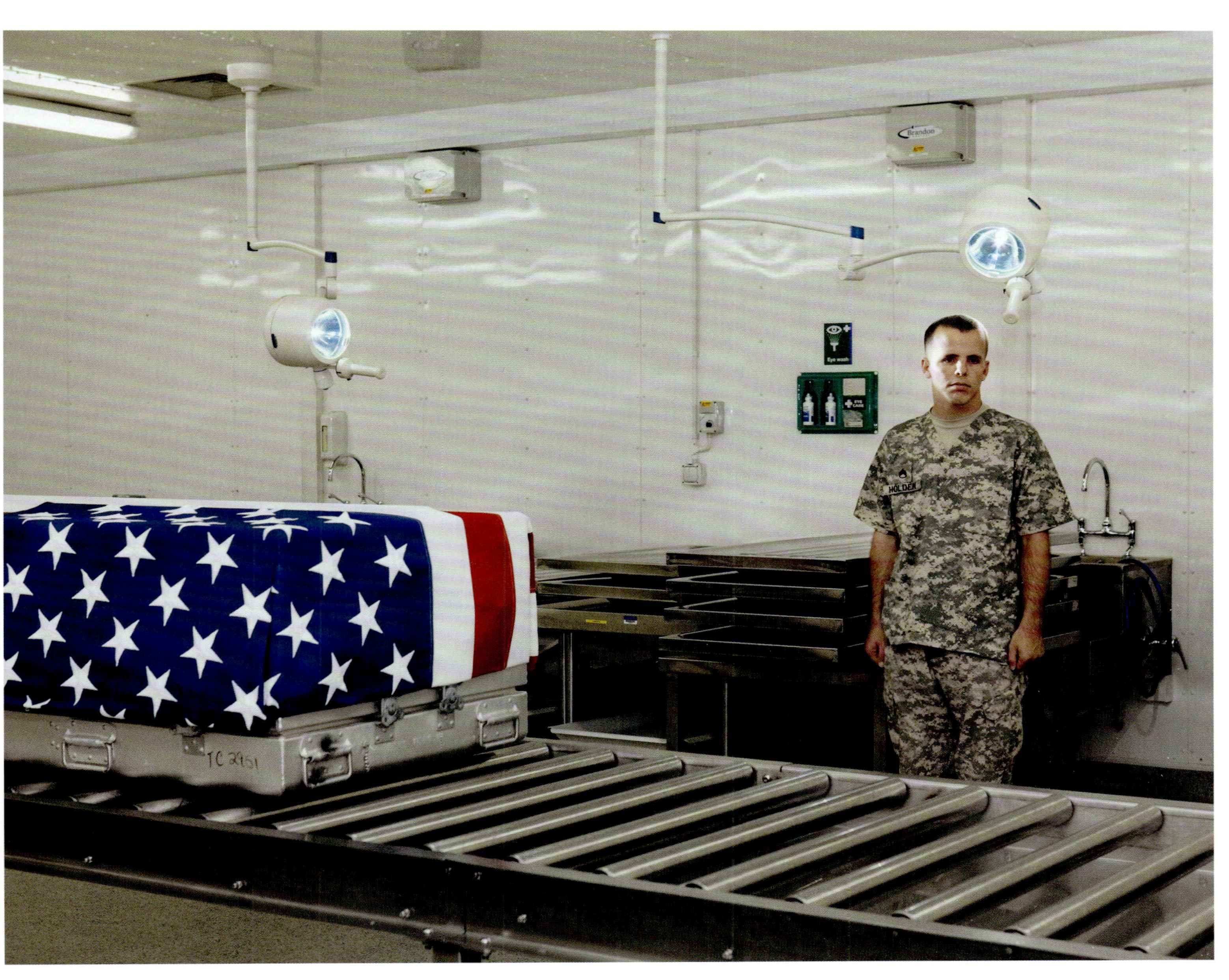

PHILIP CHEUNG
STAFF SERGEANT JEFFREY HOLDEN,
U.S. MORTUARY AFFAIRS SPECIALIST
FROM THE SERIES *SOLDIERS' ANGELS – U.S. MORTUARY AFFAIRS SPECIALISTS IN AFGHANISTAN*
JUNE 2010

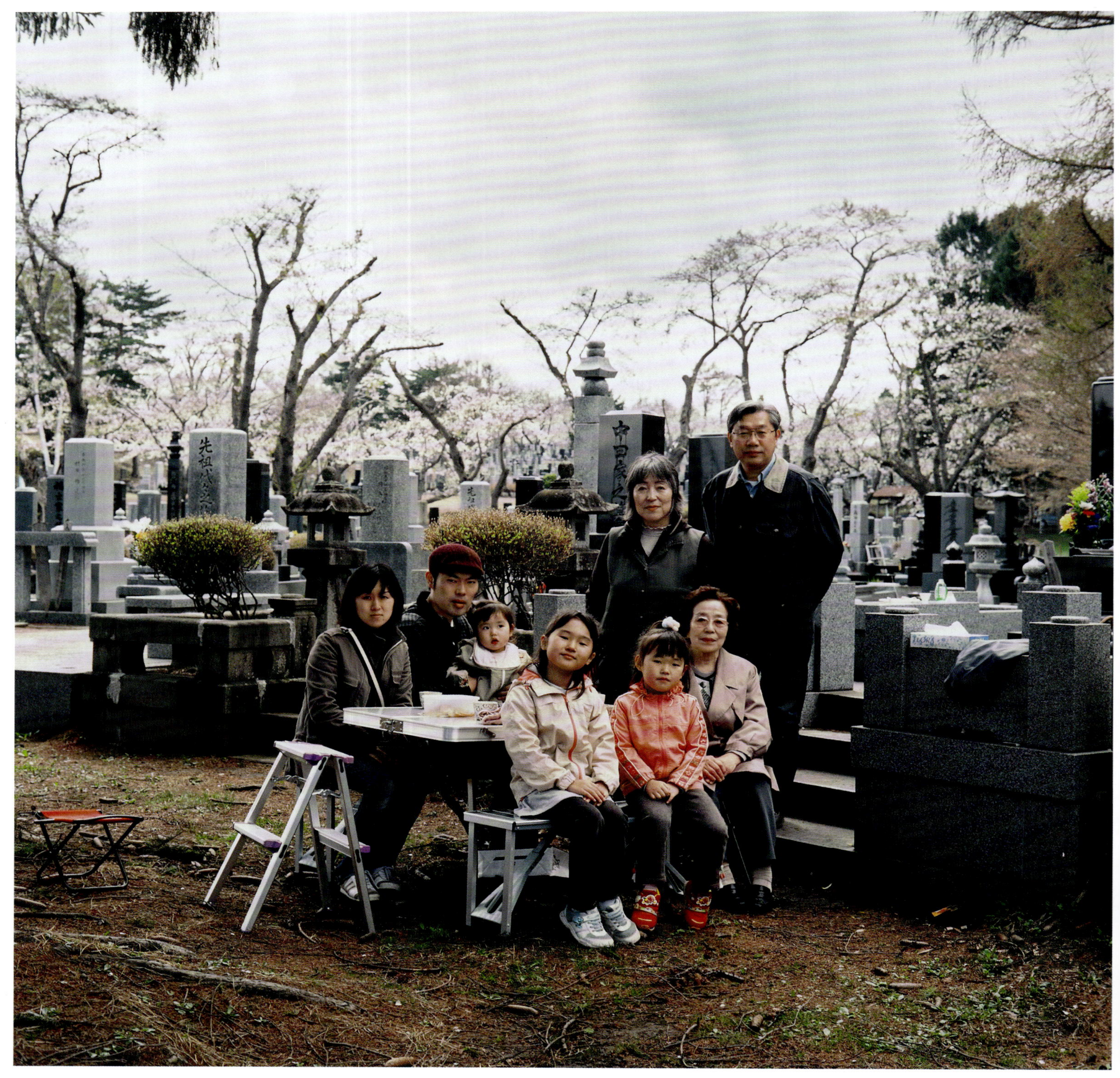

MASAYO ITO
AT THE CEMETERY 3
FROM THE SERIES *SAKURA (CHERRY BLOSSOM)*
MAY 2011

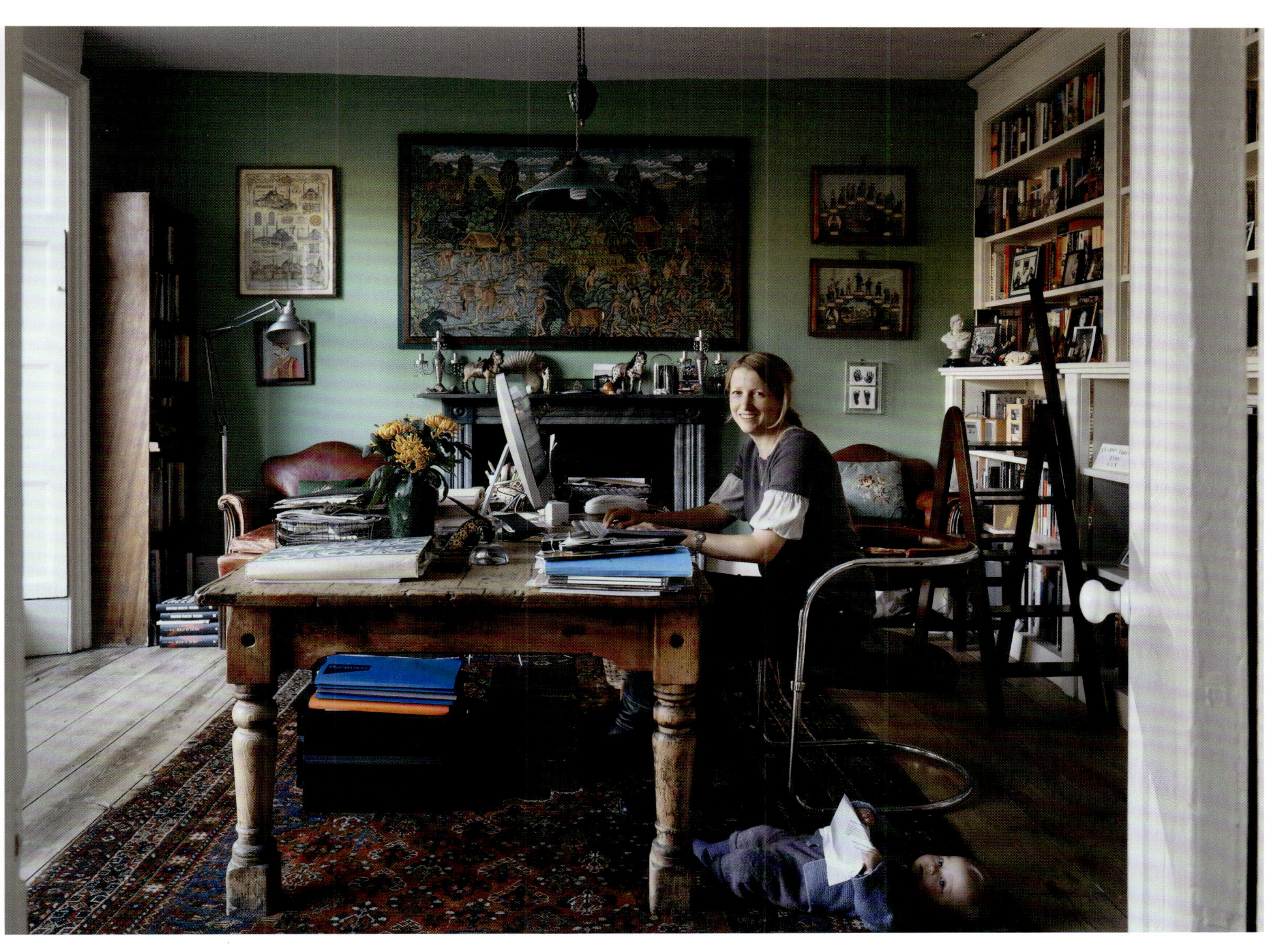

SIMON BROWN

DAISY GARNETT, JOURNALIST, AT WORK IN HER OFFICE & ROSE

DECEMBER 2010

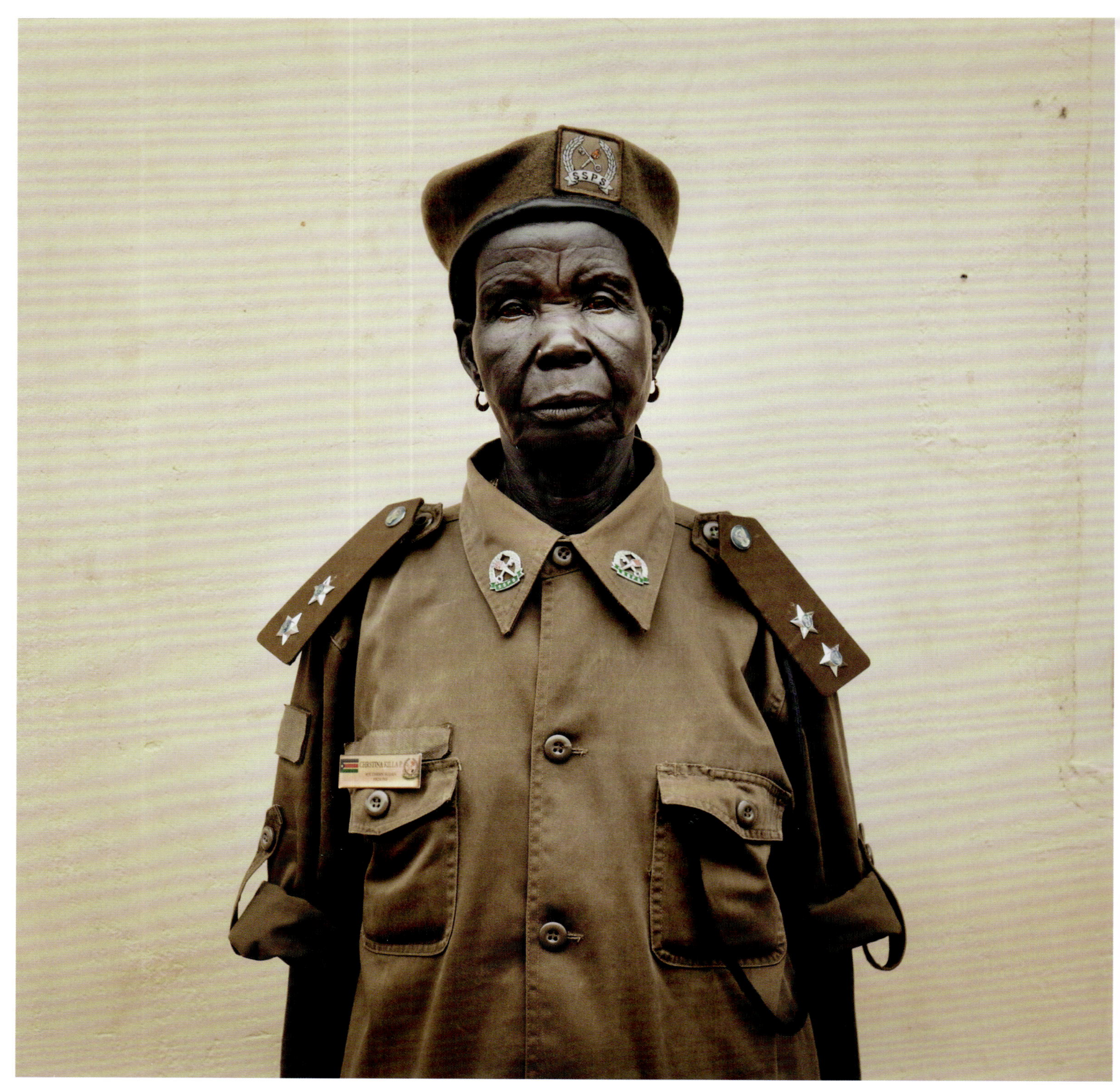

ALINKA ECHEVERRIA
CHRISTINA KILLA, CHIEF PRISON OFFICER
FROM THE SERIES *BECOMING SOUTH SUDAN*
JUNE 2011

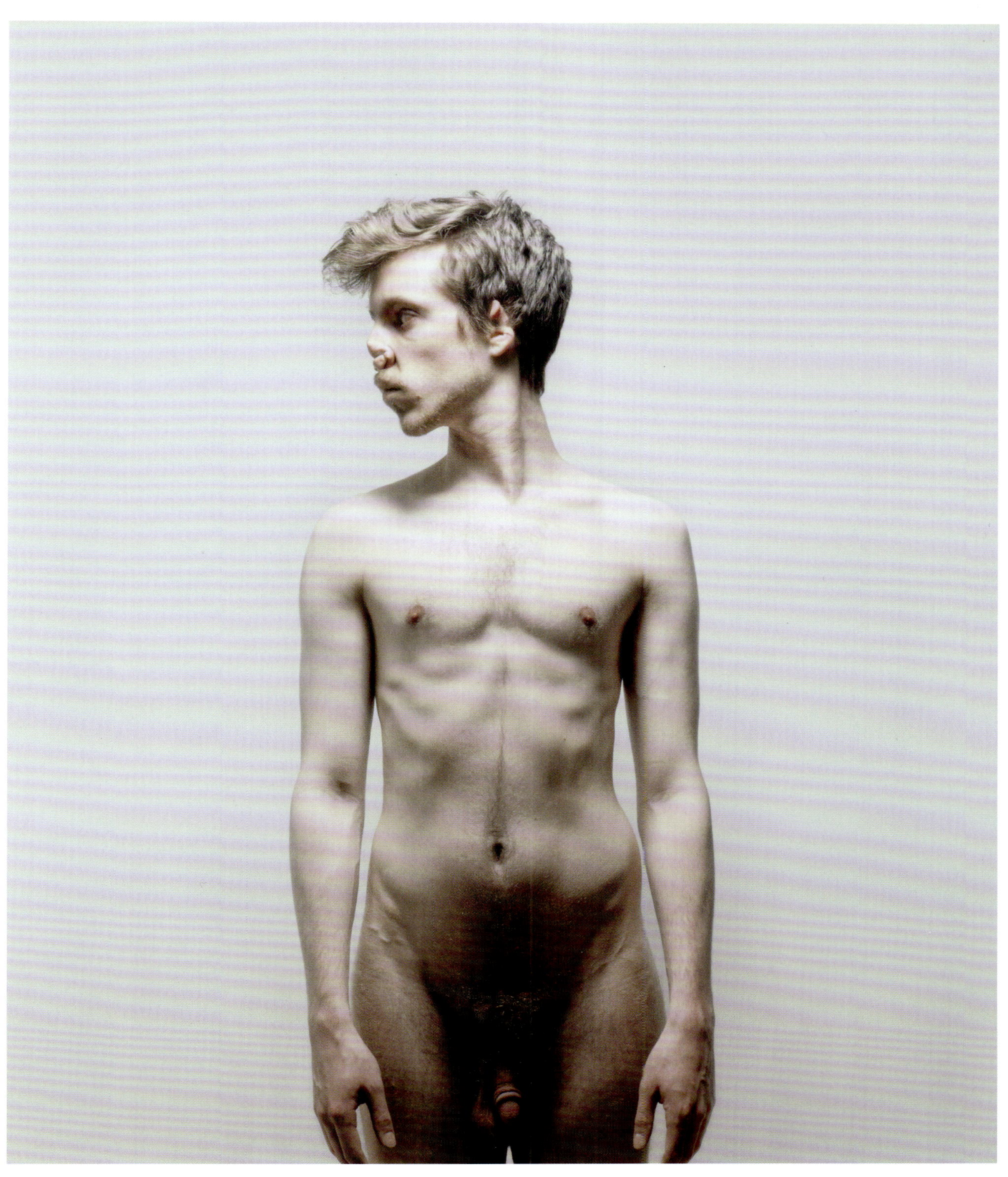

TOBIAS SLATER-HUNT
CLOSER TO GOD XVII
FROM THE SERIES *CLOSER TO GOD*
FEBRUARY 2011

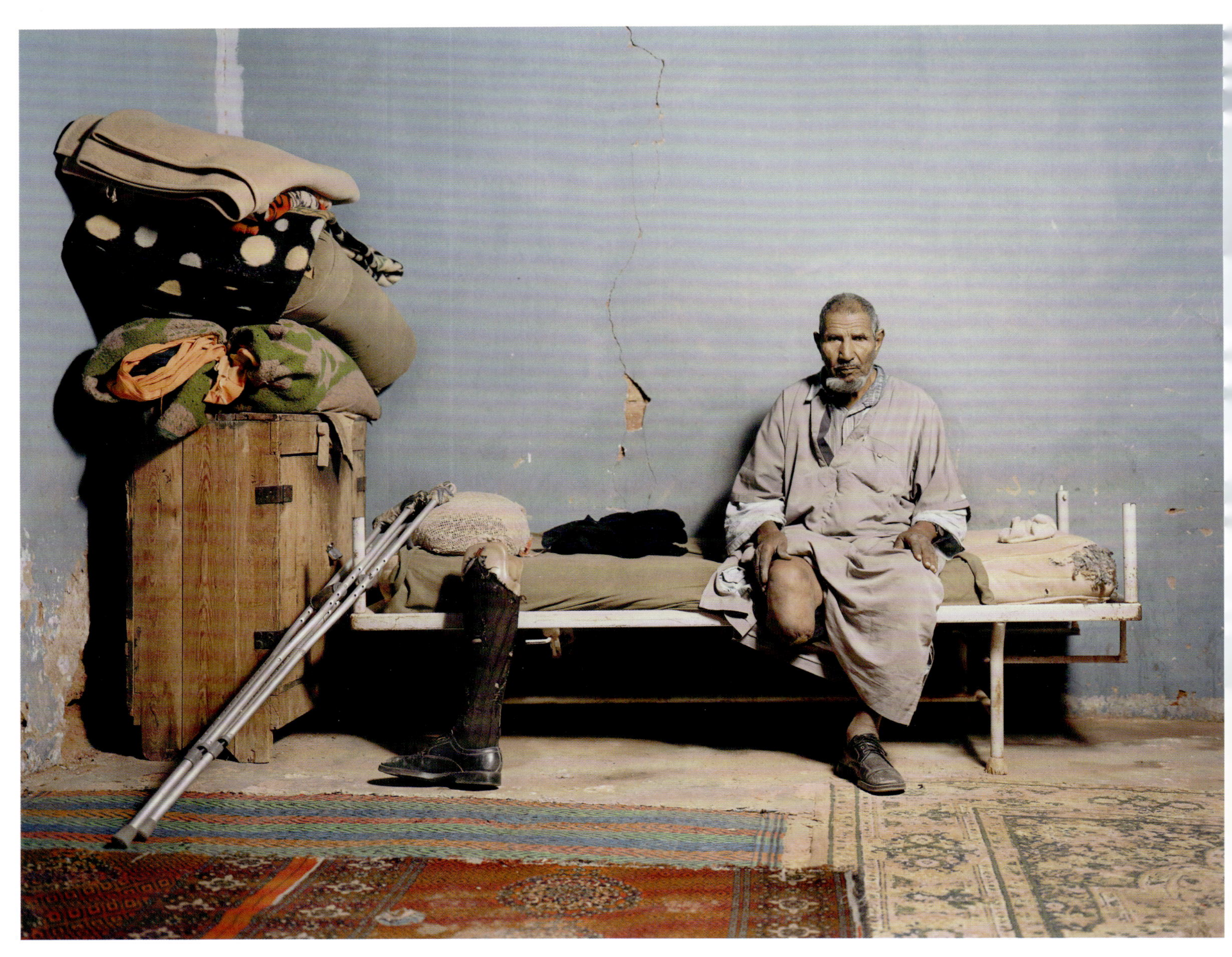

BERNAT MILLET
SIDIAJMED EMBARJ BRICK
FROM THE SERIES *SAHARAWIS*
JANUARY 2011

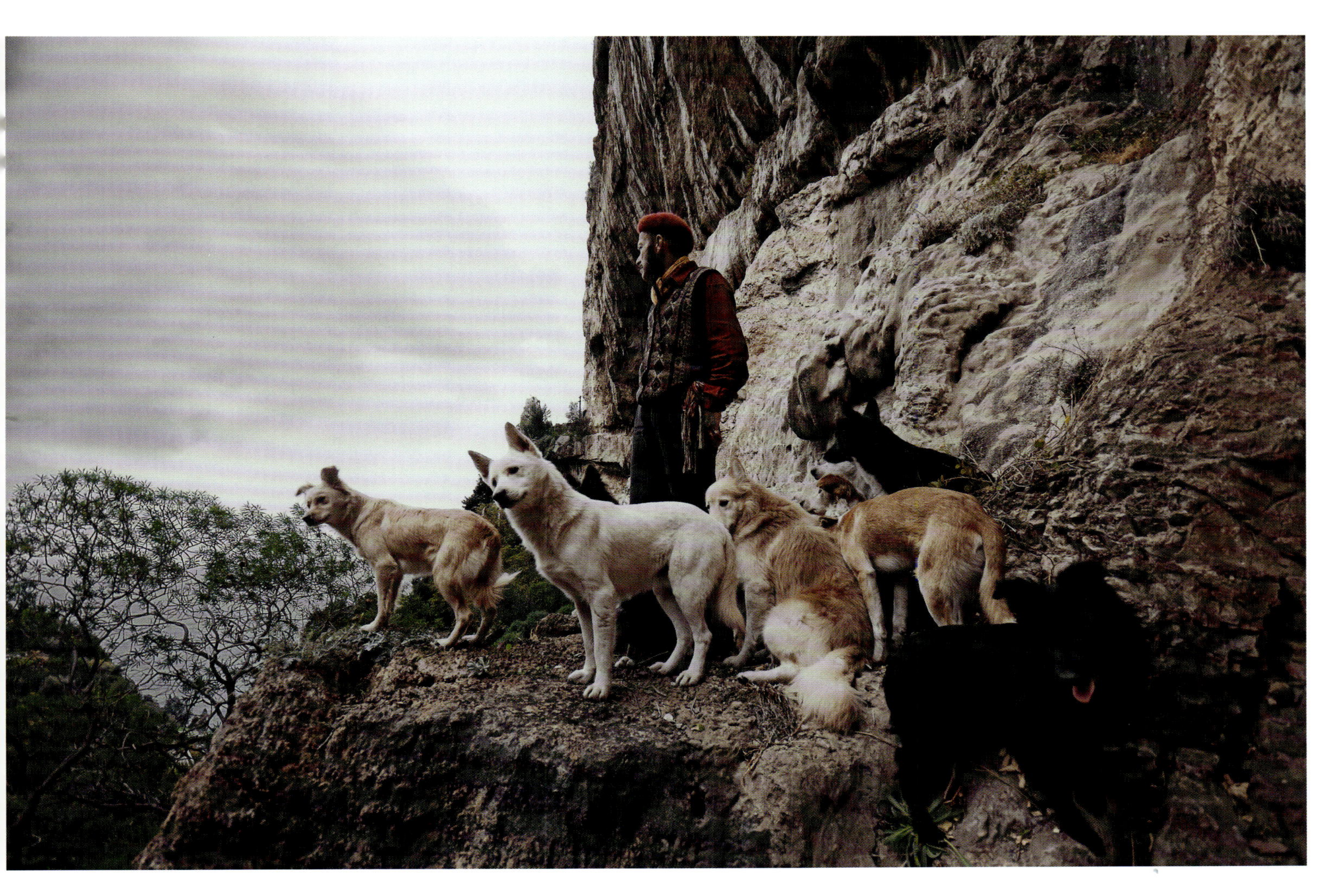

CARLO BEVILACQUA
GIANNI HERMIT FOR LOVE
FROM THE SERIES *INTO THE SILENCE*
NOVEMBER 2010

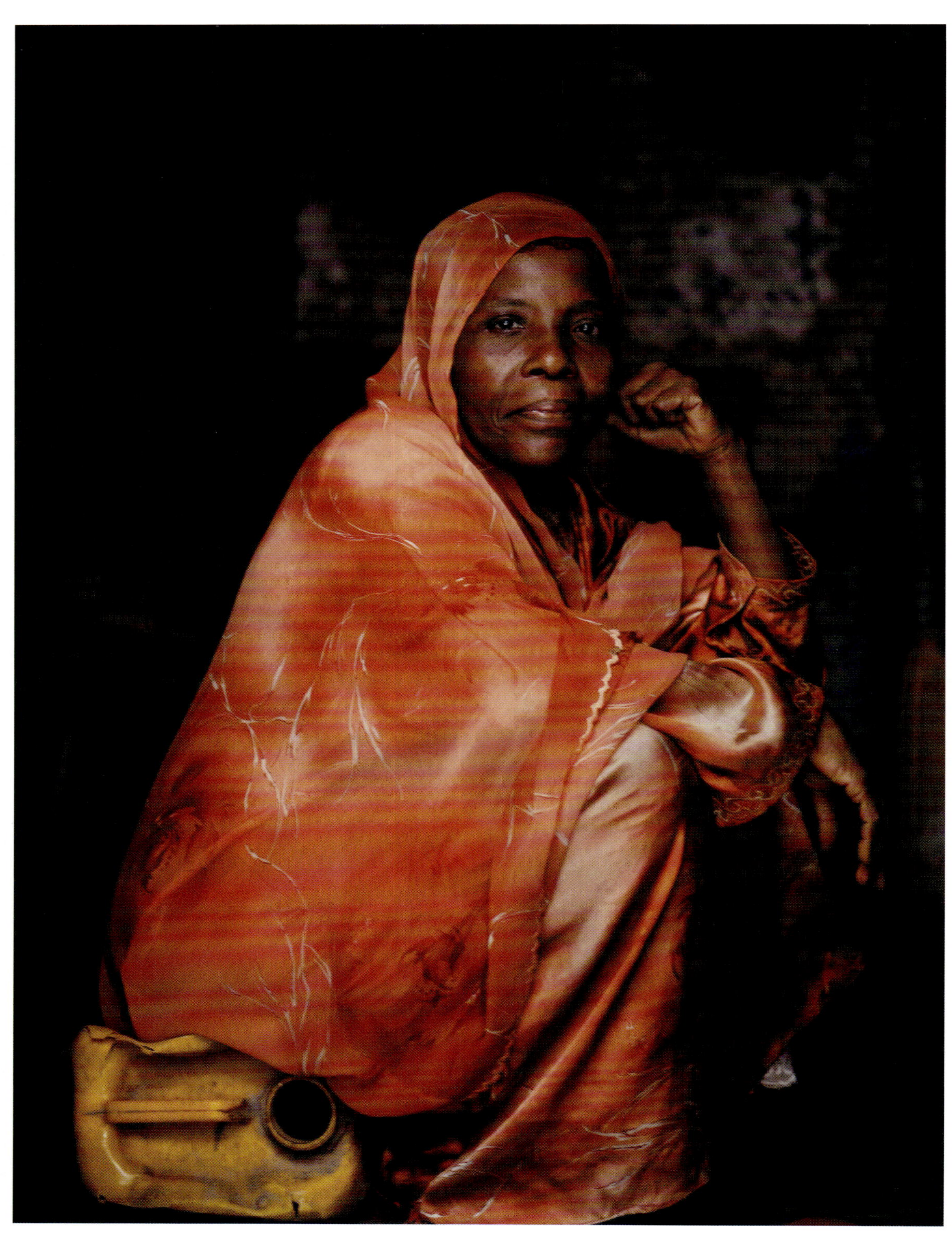

NICK RILEY
WOMAN IN ORANGE
JANUARY 2010

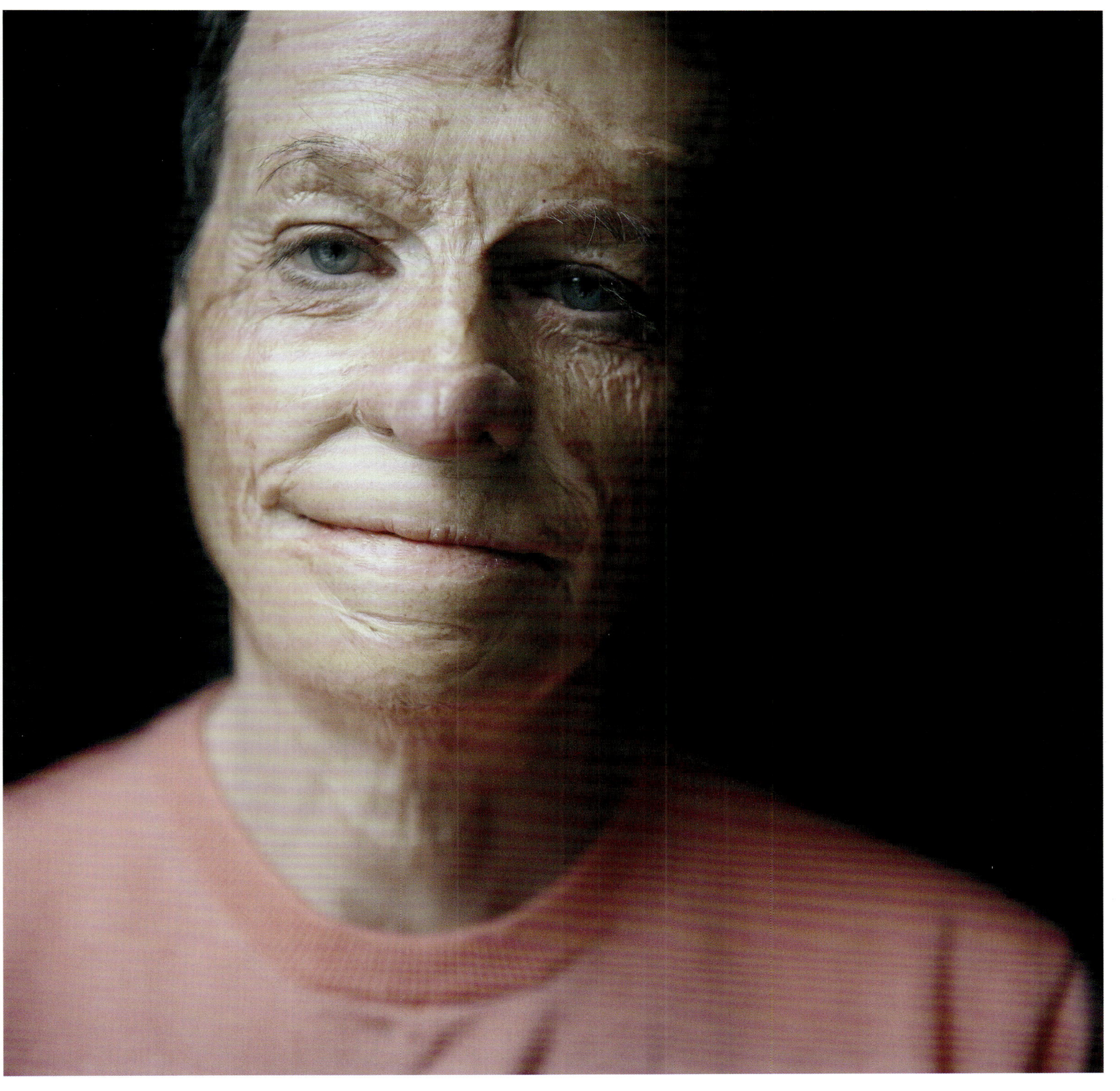

MARK JOHNSON
LEO GORMLEY
FROM THE SERIES *THE UGLY FACE OF PREJUDICE*
NOVEMBER 2010

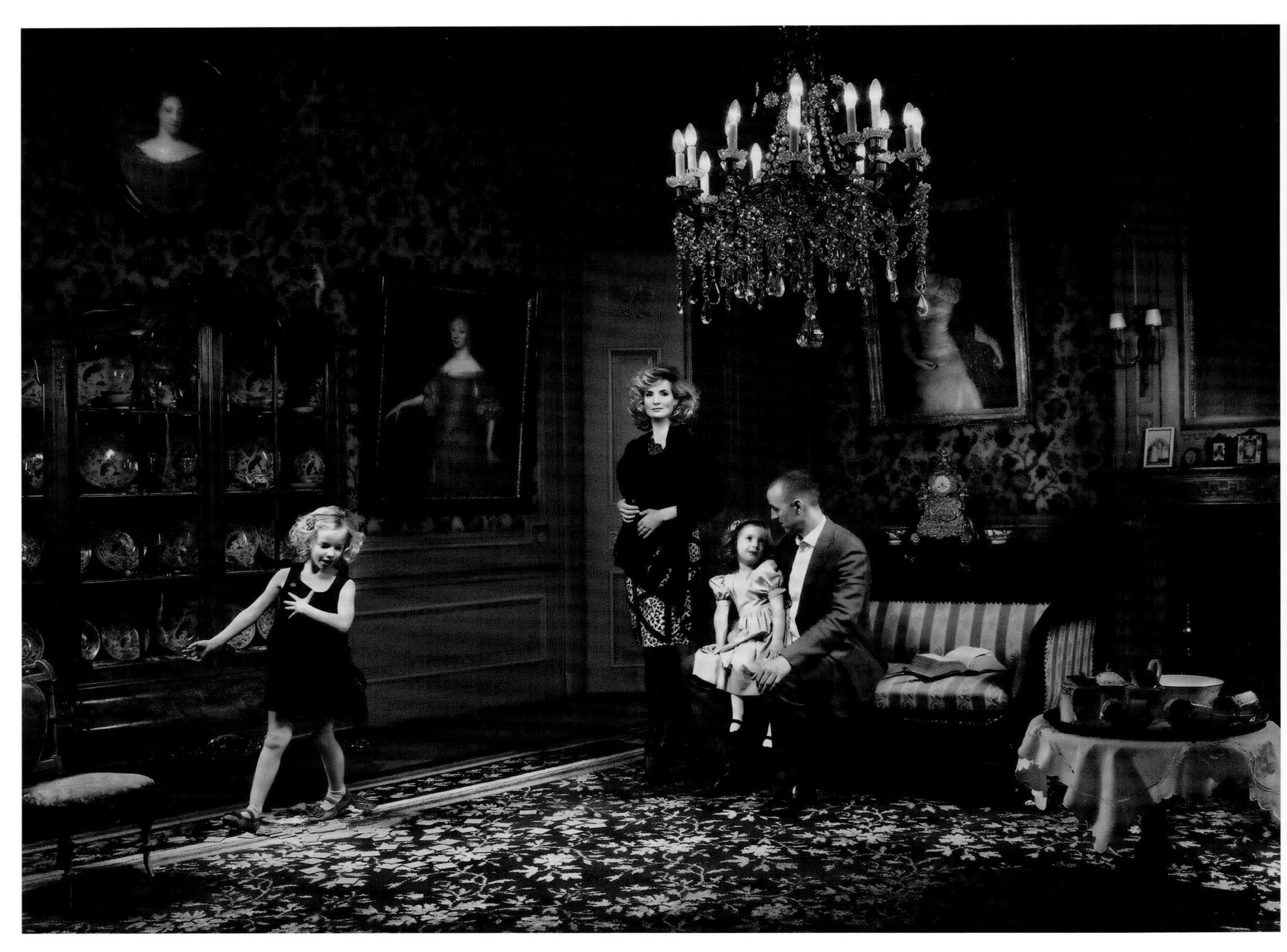

ILYA VAN MARLE
FAMILY PORTRAIT VAN DER BORCH VAN VERWOLDE
FROM THE SERIES *A FAMILY PORTRAIT*
FEBRUARY 2011

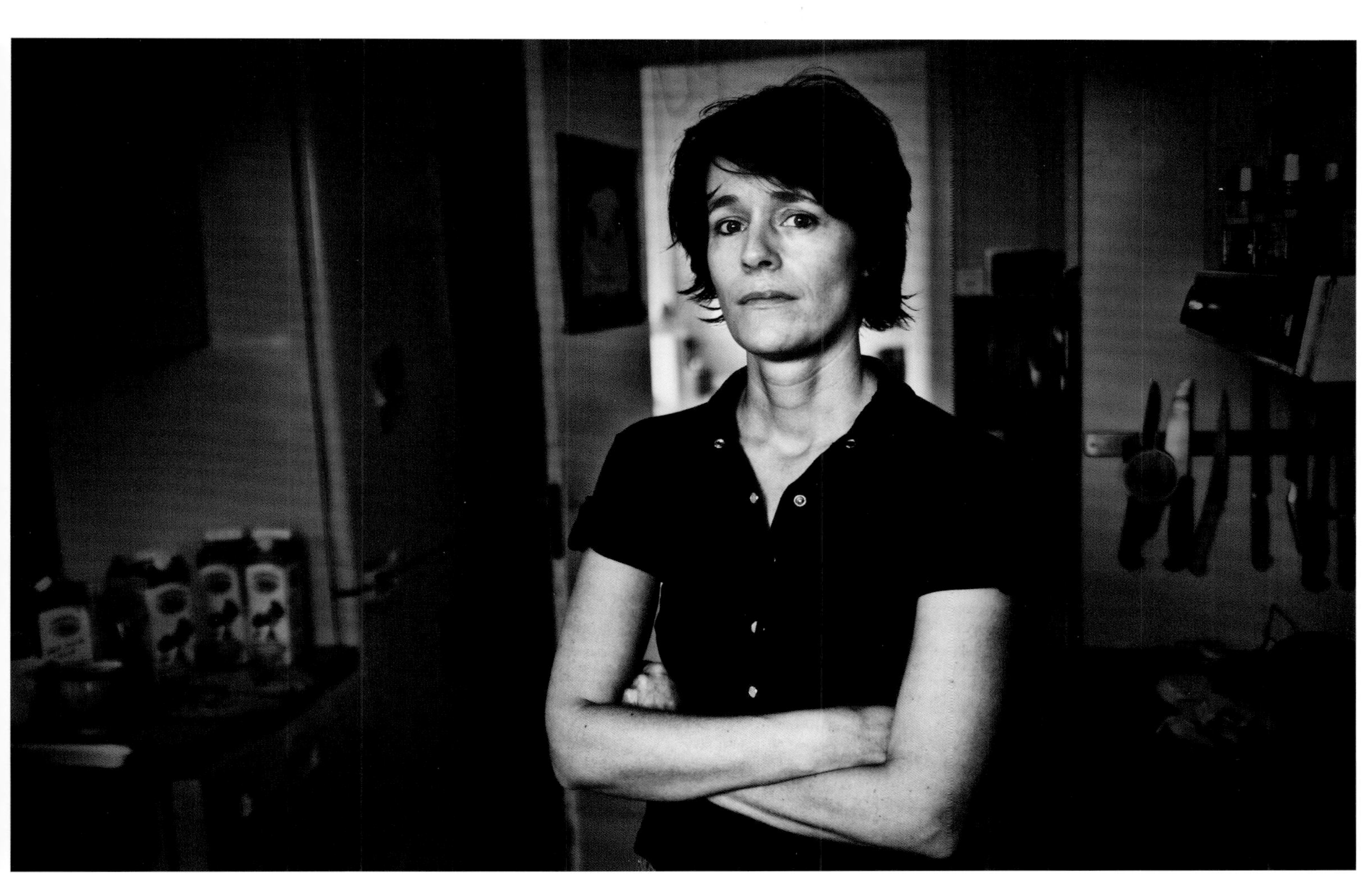

TORBEN ÅNDAHL
EIKE
FROM THE SERIES *THE BEREAVED*
JUNE 2010

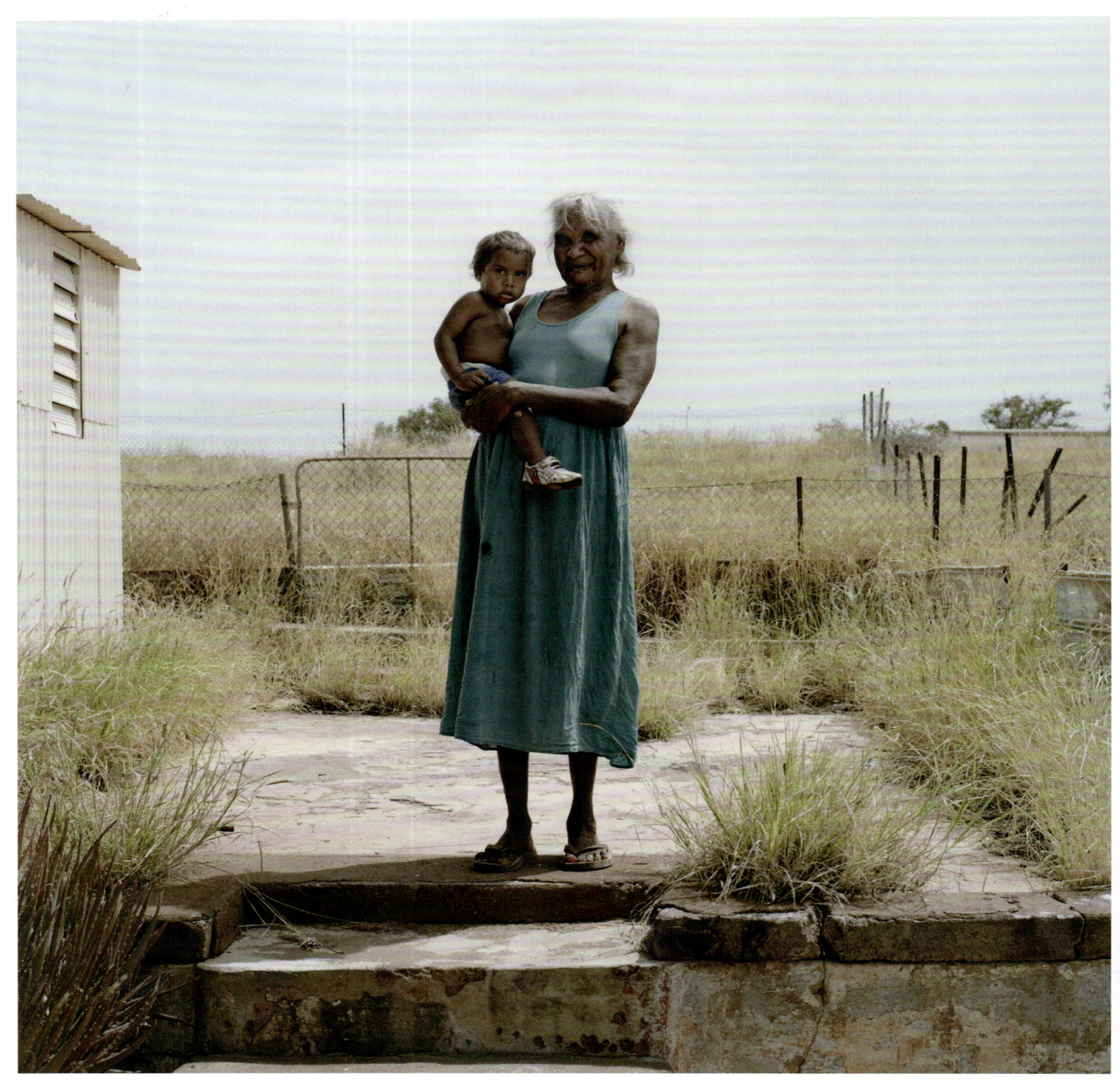

CLAUDIO RASANO
TRUST OF ABORIGINAL AUSTRALIA
FEBRUARY 2010

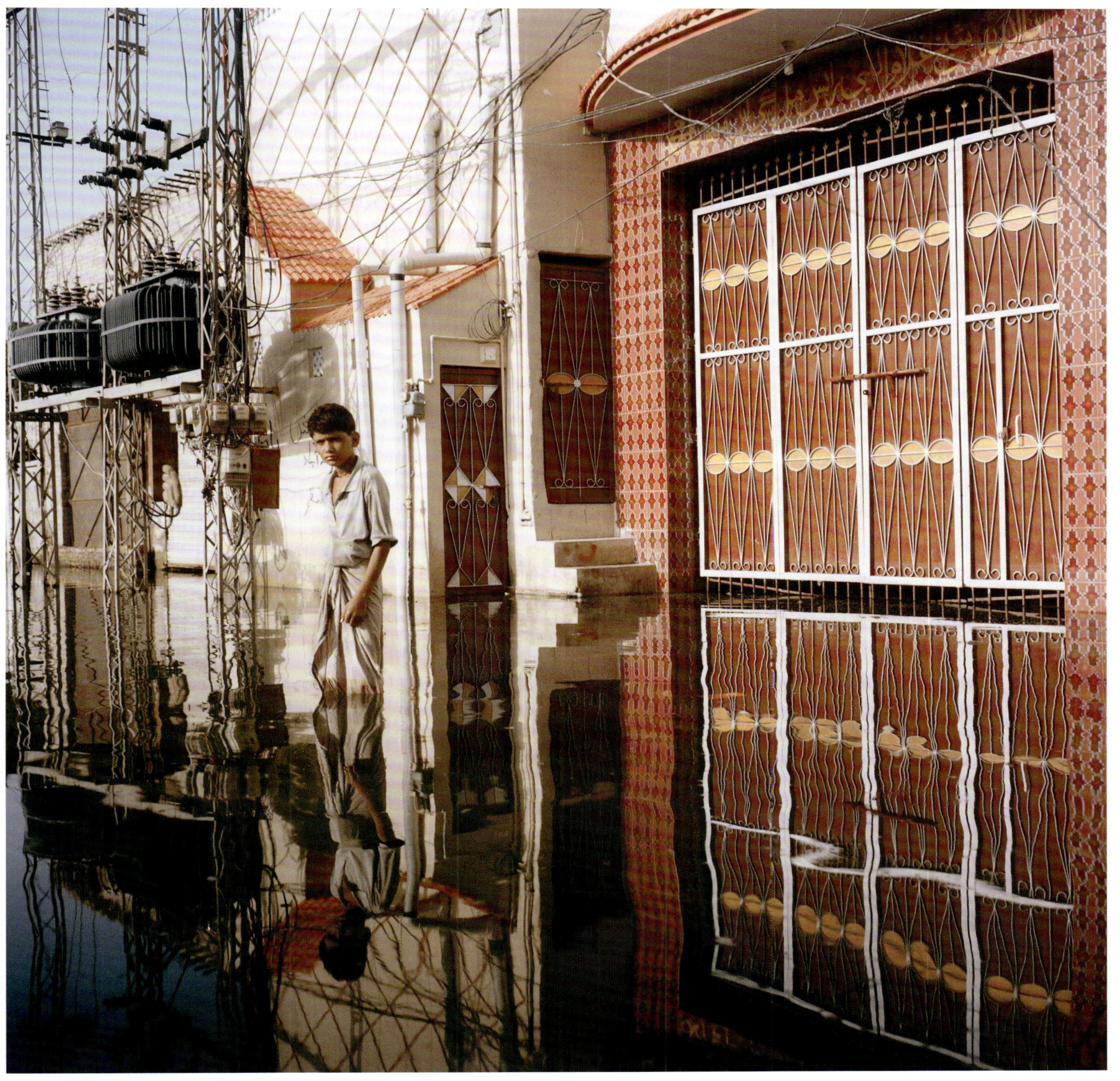

GIDEON MENDEL
PORTRAIT OF ASIF IN THE FLOODED TOWN OF KHAIRPUR NATHAN SHAH
FROM THE SERIES *DROWNING WORLD/PAKISTAN FLOODS*
FOR *ACTIONAID* AND THE *GUARDIAN WEEKEND* MAGAZINE
SEPTEMBER 2010

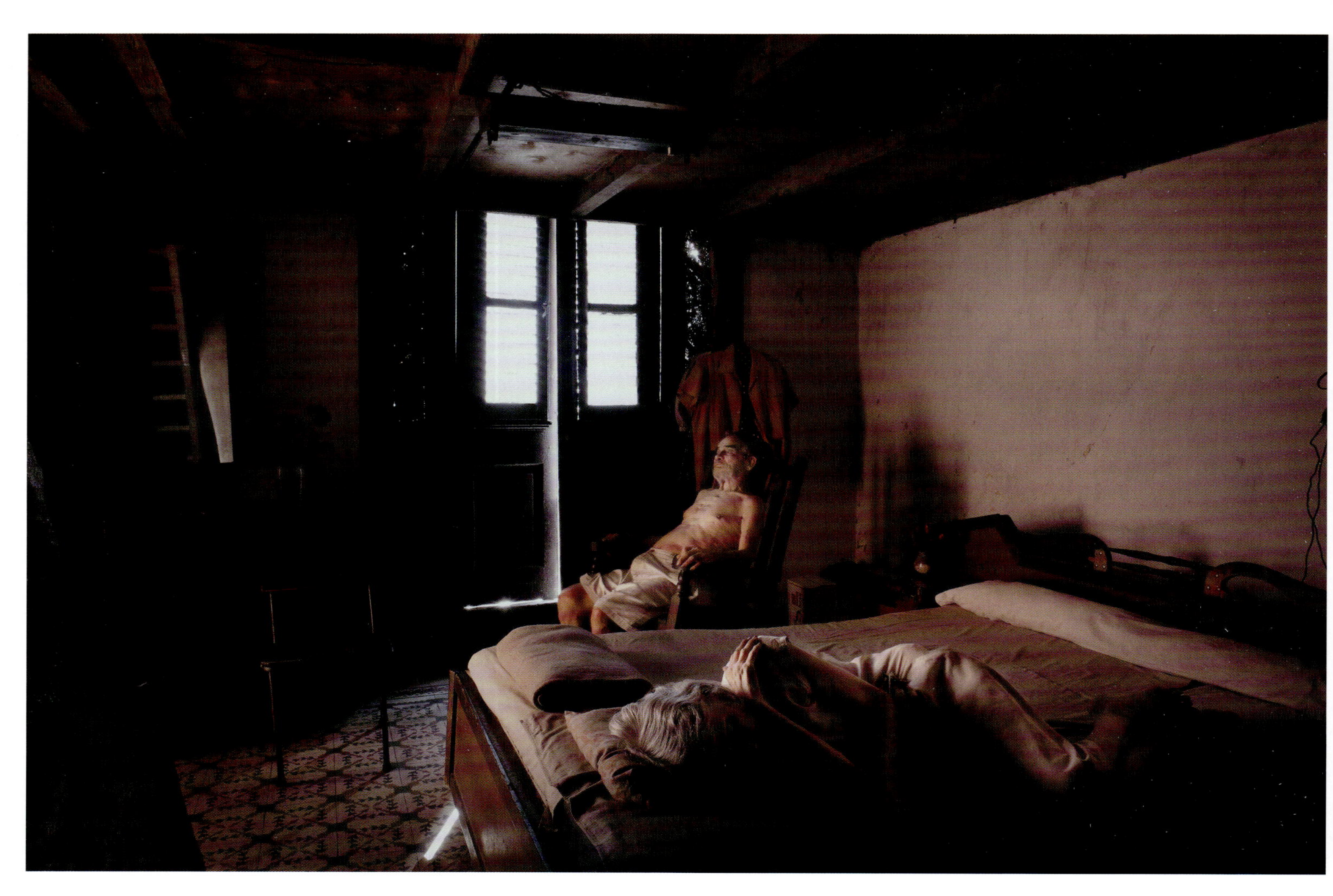

DAVID CREEDON
MARIA AND RAUL, PASO MARTI, CENTRO HABANO
JUNE 2011

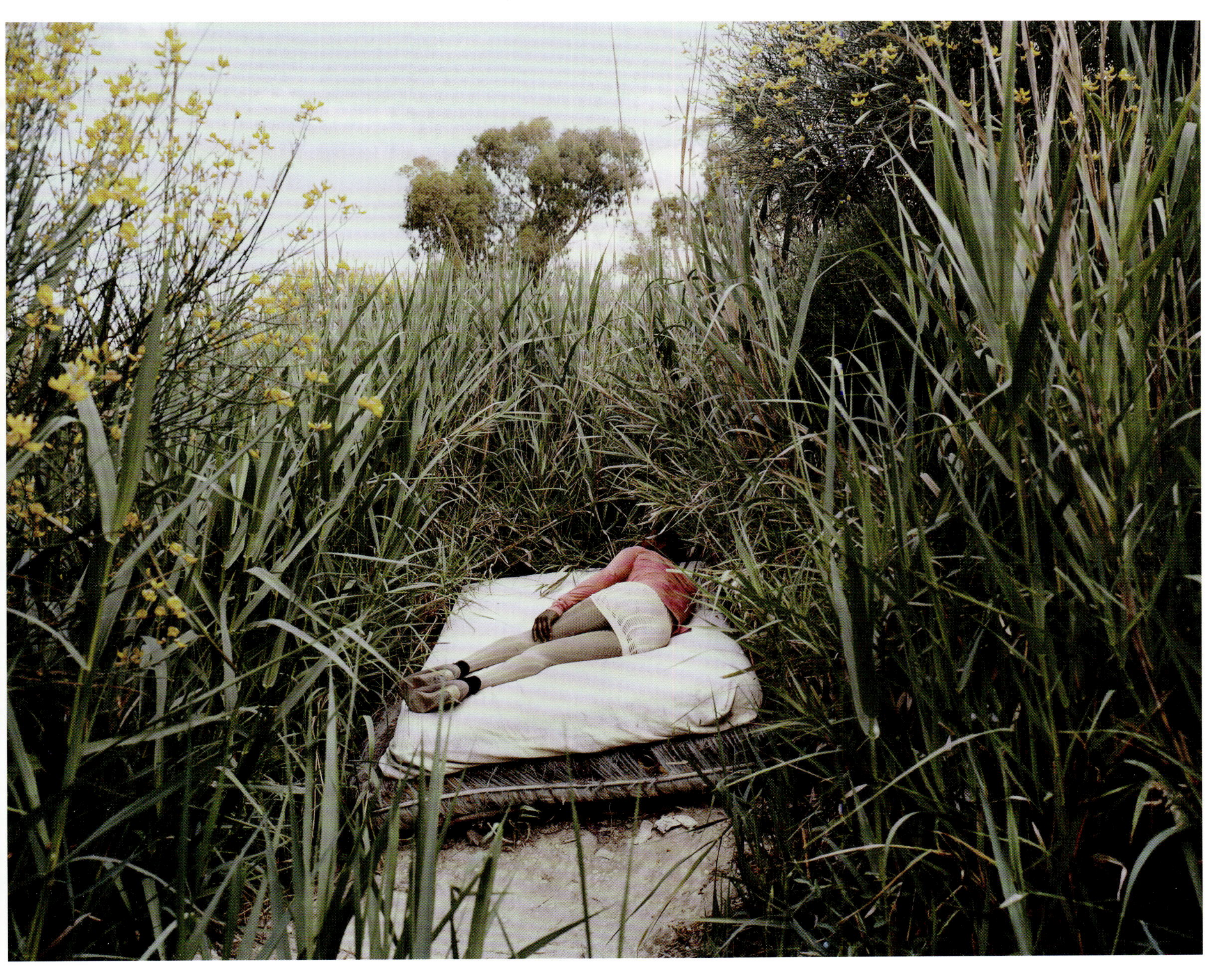

PAOLO PATRIZI
ANNA
FROM THE SERIES *MIGRATION LINKED TO PROSTITUTION*
MARCH 2010

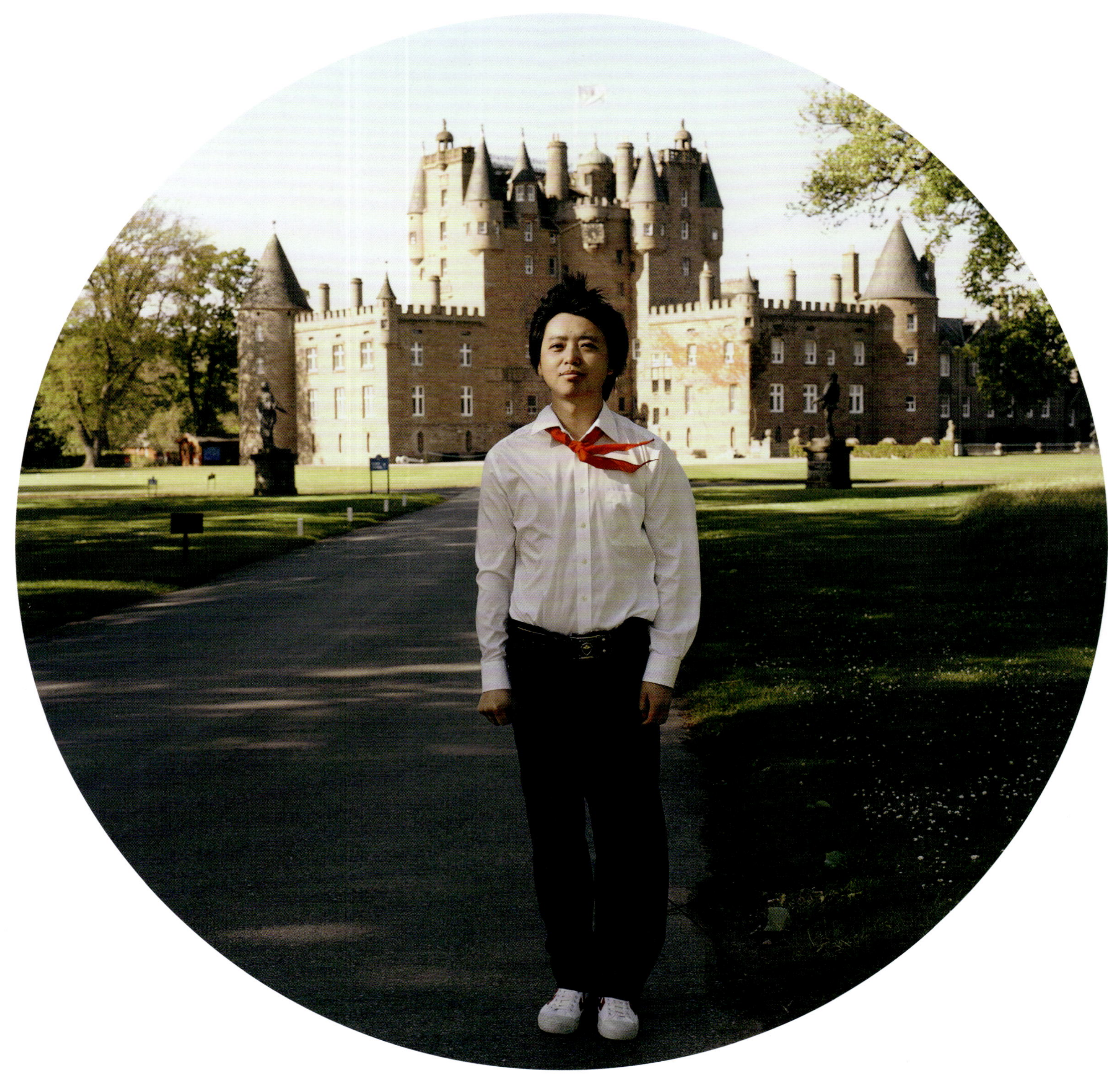

HUI YAO
GLAMIS CASTLE, ANGUS, UK
FROM THE SERIES *MIRAGE*
MAY 2011

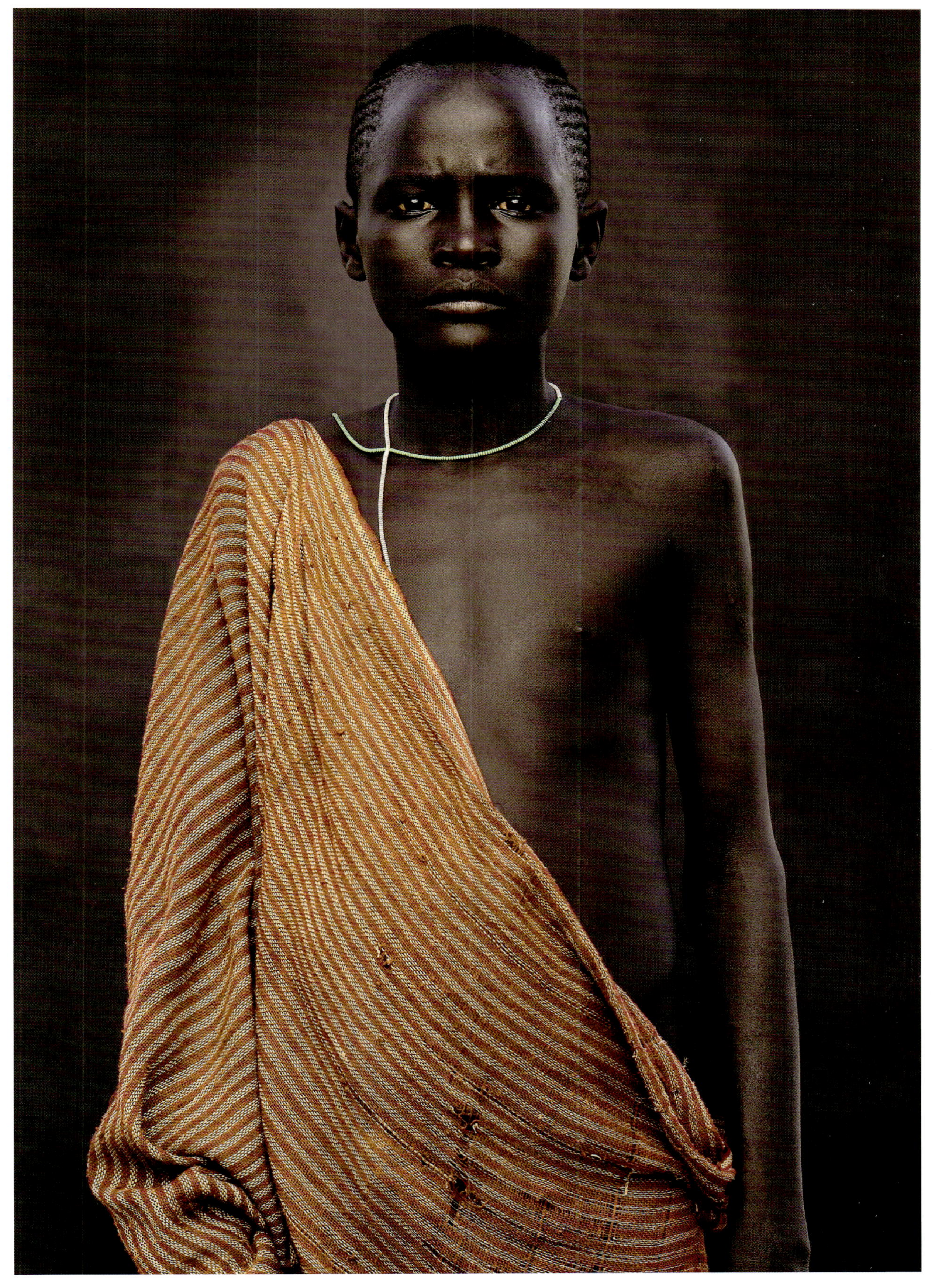

MARIO MARINO
MALEGA, SURMA BOY, ETHIOPIA, APRIL 2011
FROM THE SERIES *FACES OF AFRICA*
APRIL 2011

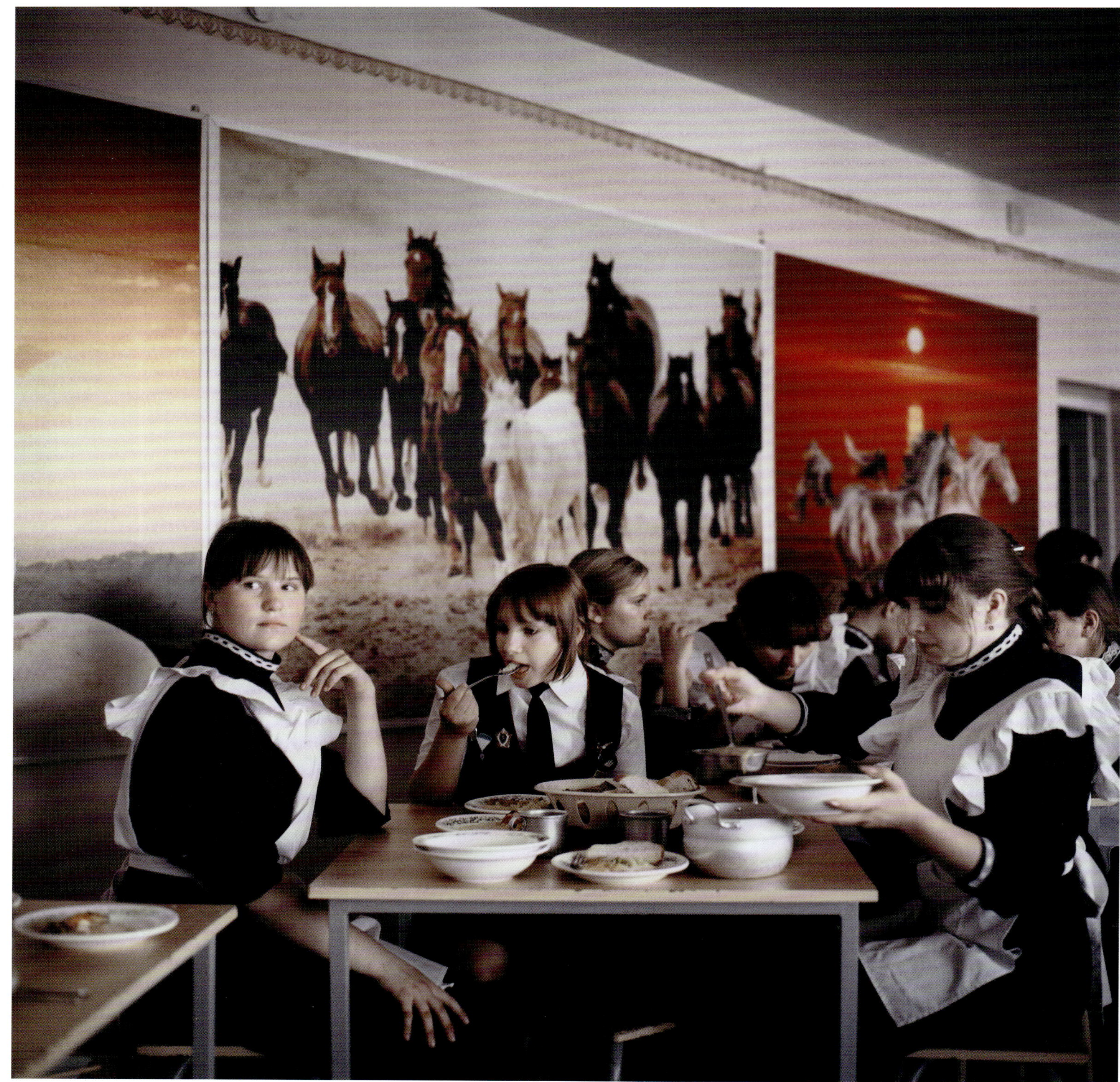

ANASTASIA TAYLOR-LIND

LUCIA SHABAEVA AND HER YEAR 9 CLASSMATES, WHO ARE ALL BETWEEN 15 AND 16 YEARS OLD, DURING LUNCH IN THE CANTEEN OF ATAMAN PLATOV COSSACK CADET SCHOOL IN BELAYA KALITVA, SOUTHERN RUSSIA
FROM THE SERIES *WOMEN OF THE COSSACK RESURGENCE*
MAY 2010

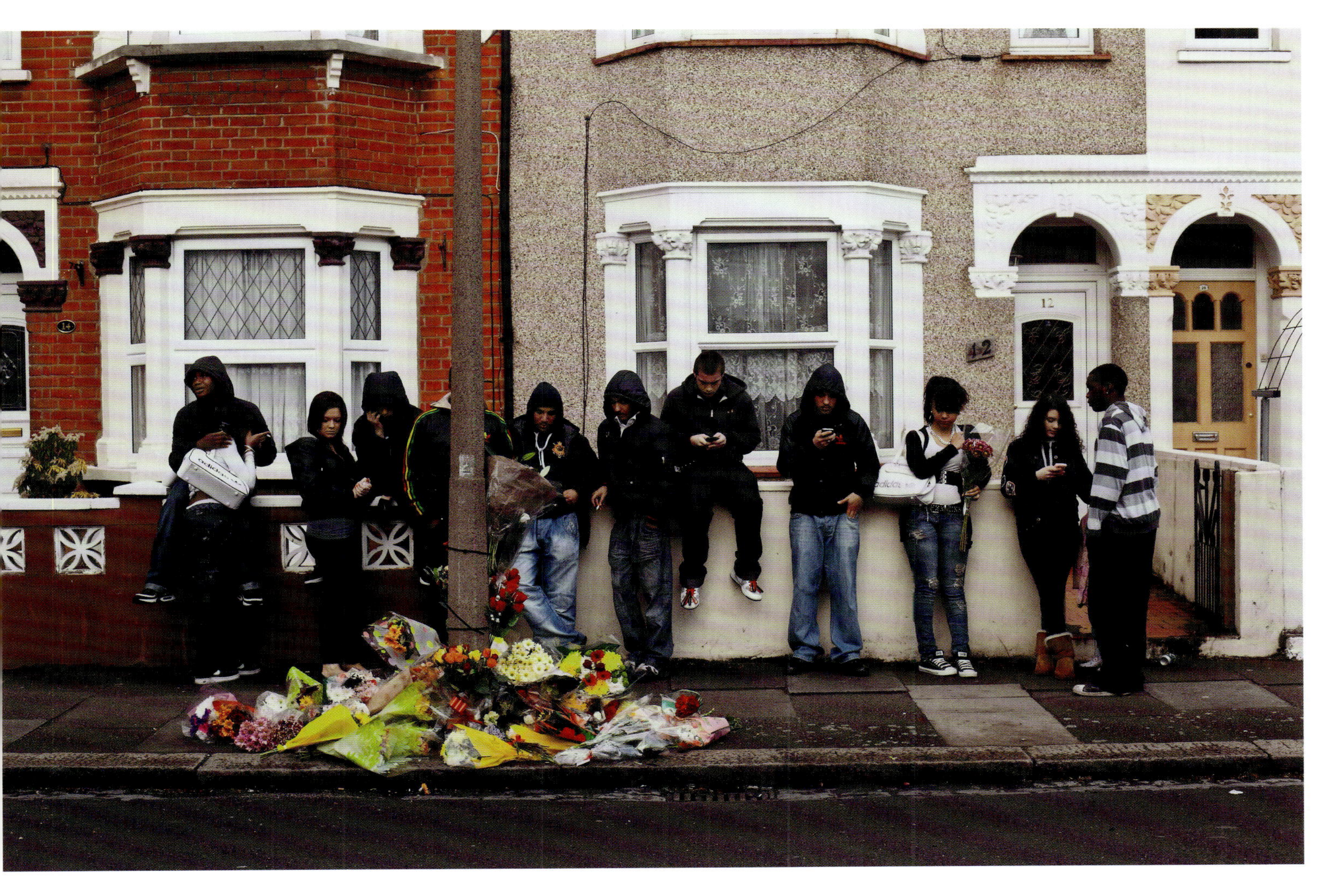

ANTONIO OLMOS
FRIENDS MOURN NEGUS MCCLEAN
APRIL 2011

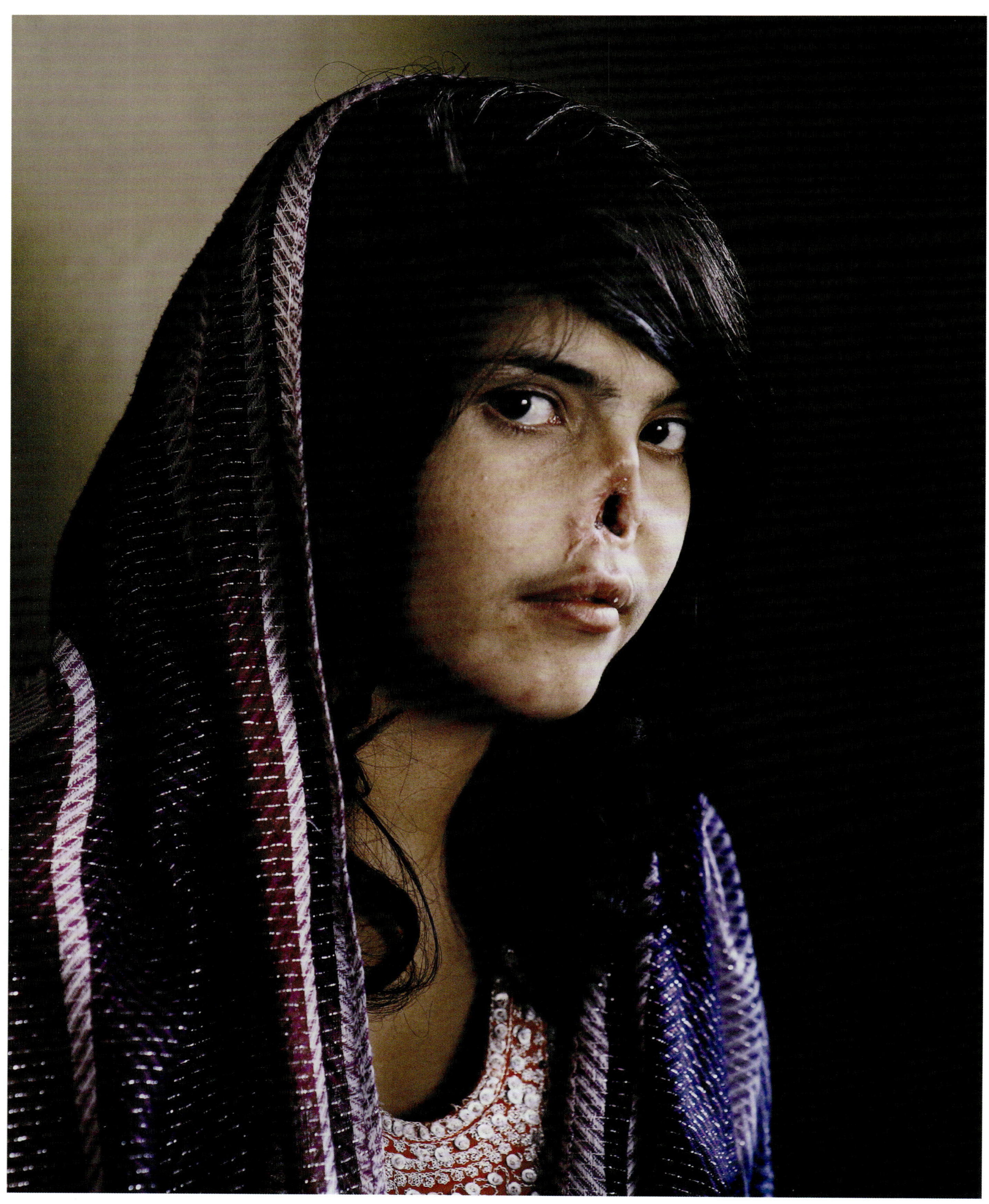

JODI BIEBER
BIBI AISHA
JULY 2010

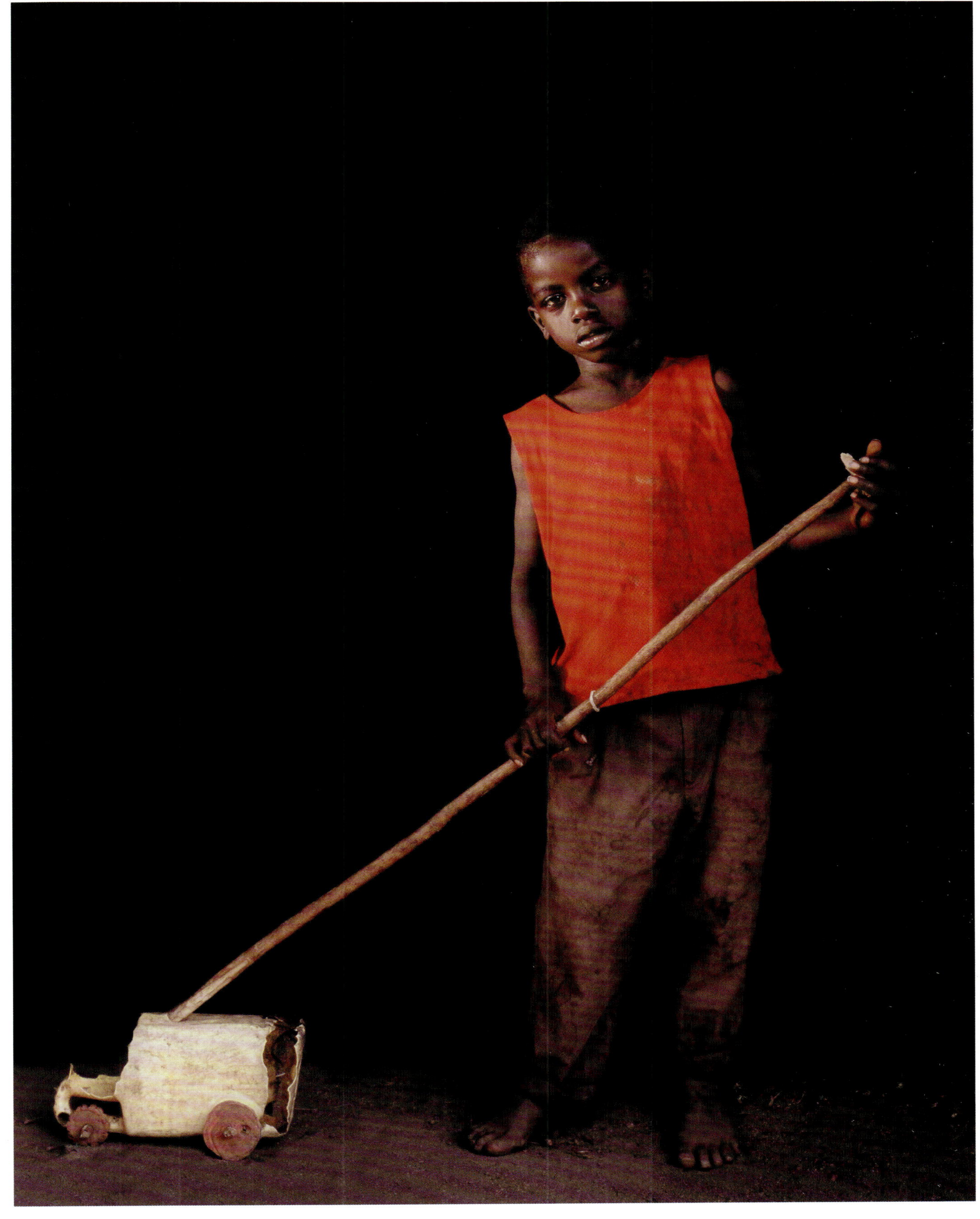

HARRY HOOK
ABENTHER, ARI BOY WITH TOY CAR
FROM THE SERIES *AFRICA STUDIO*
APRIL 2011

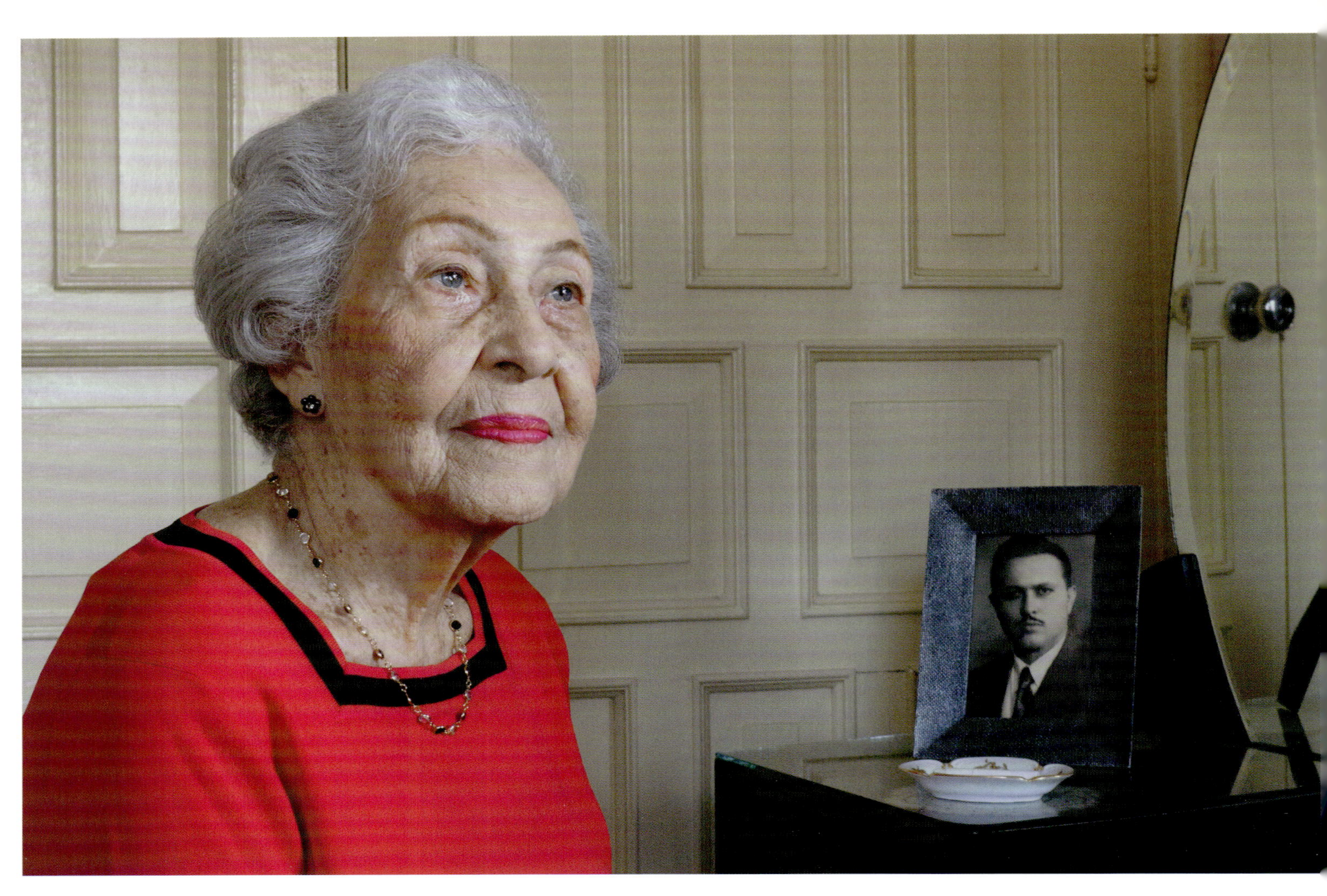

FRANK BALBI HANSEN
LOLA'S HUSBAND
SEPTEMBER 2010

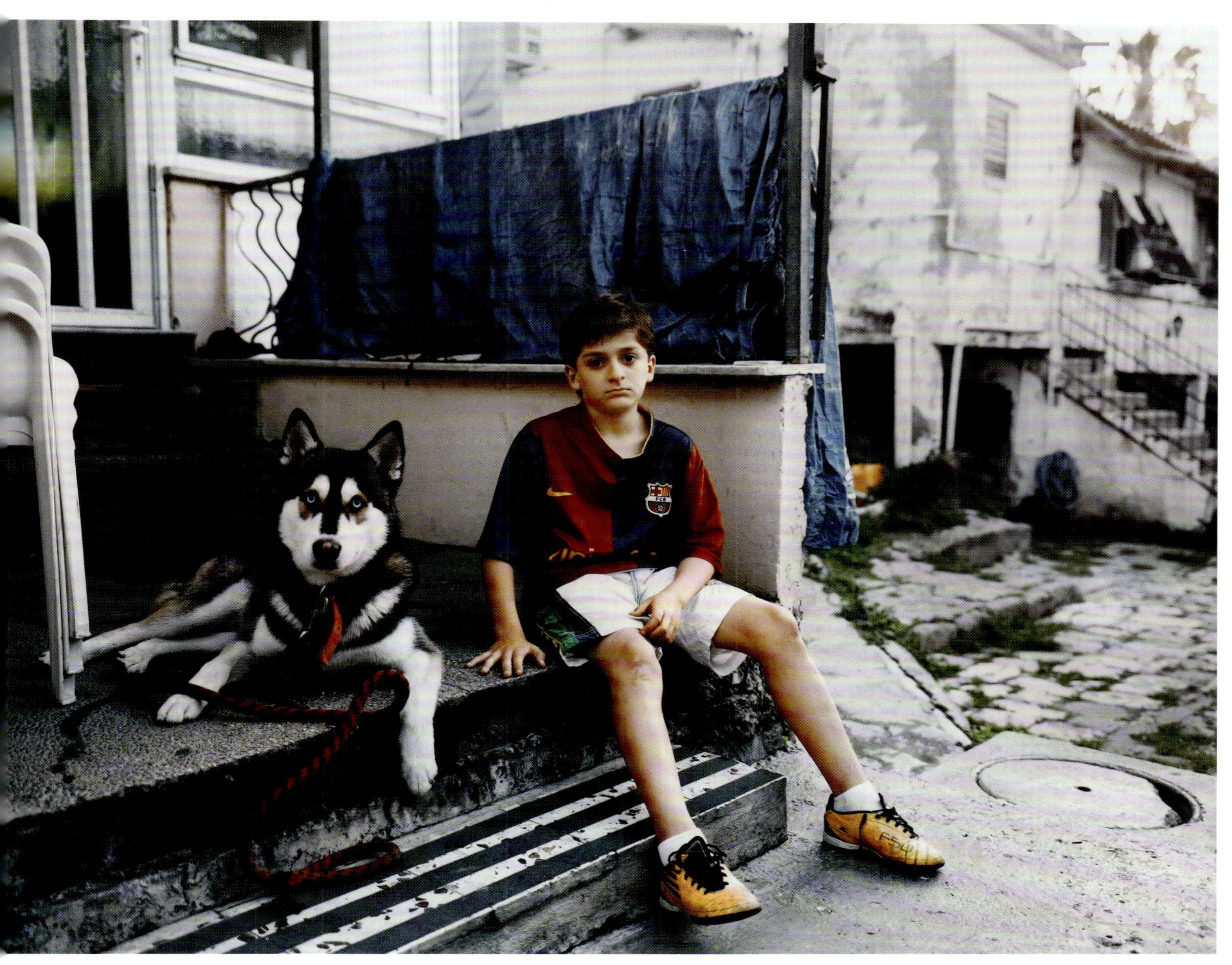

ZIV KATZ
JOHNNY
MAY 2011

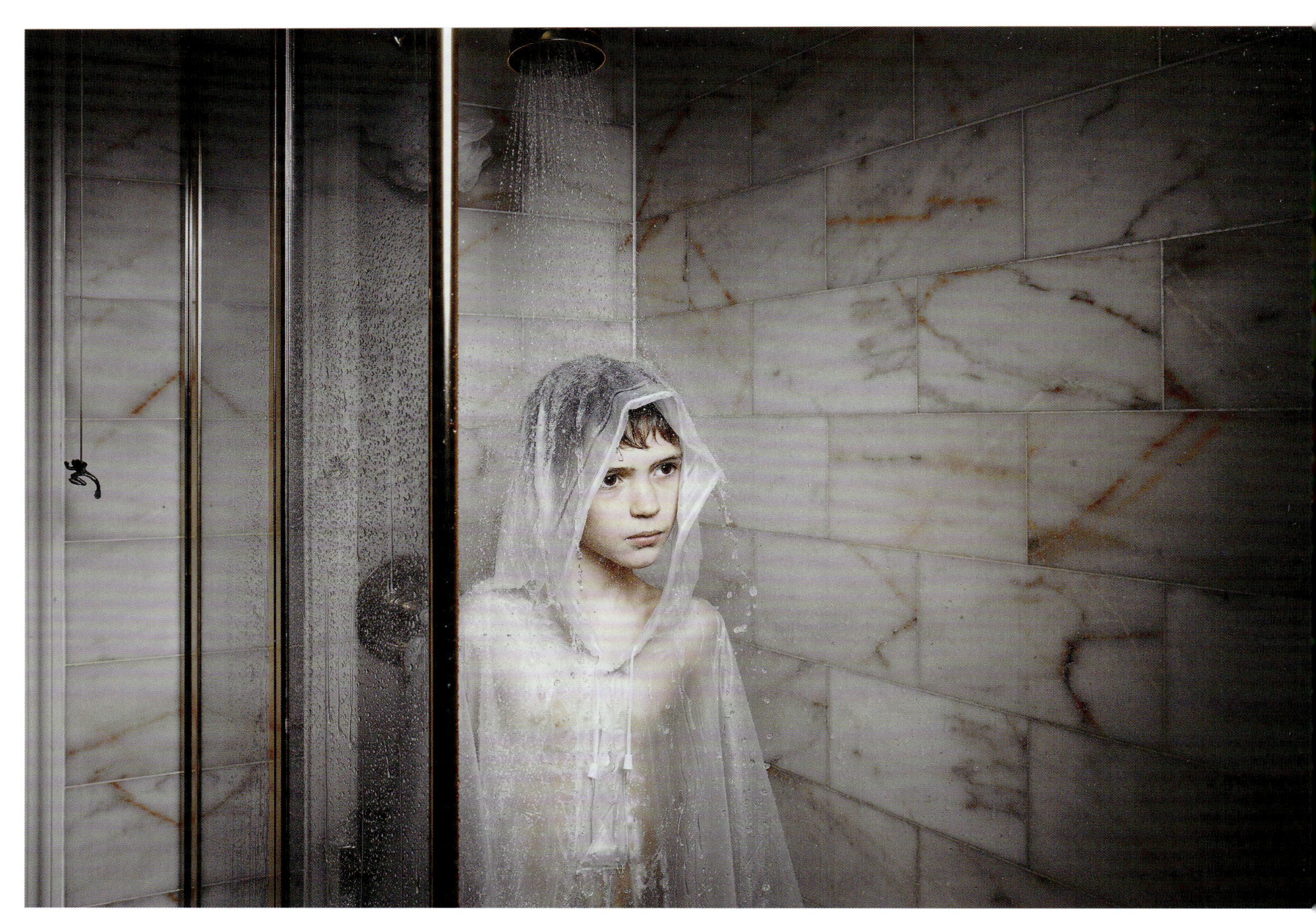

KELVIN MURRAY
OLIVER
NOVEMBER 2010

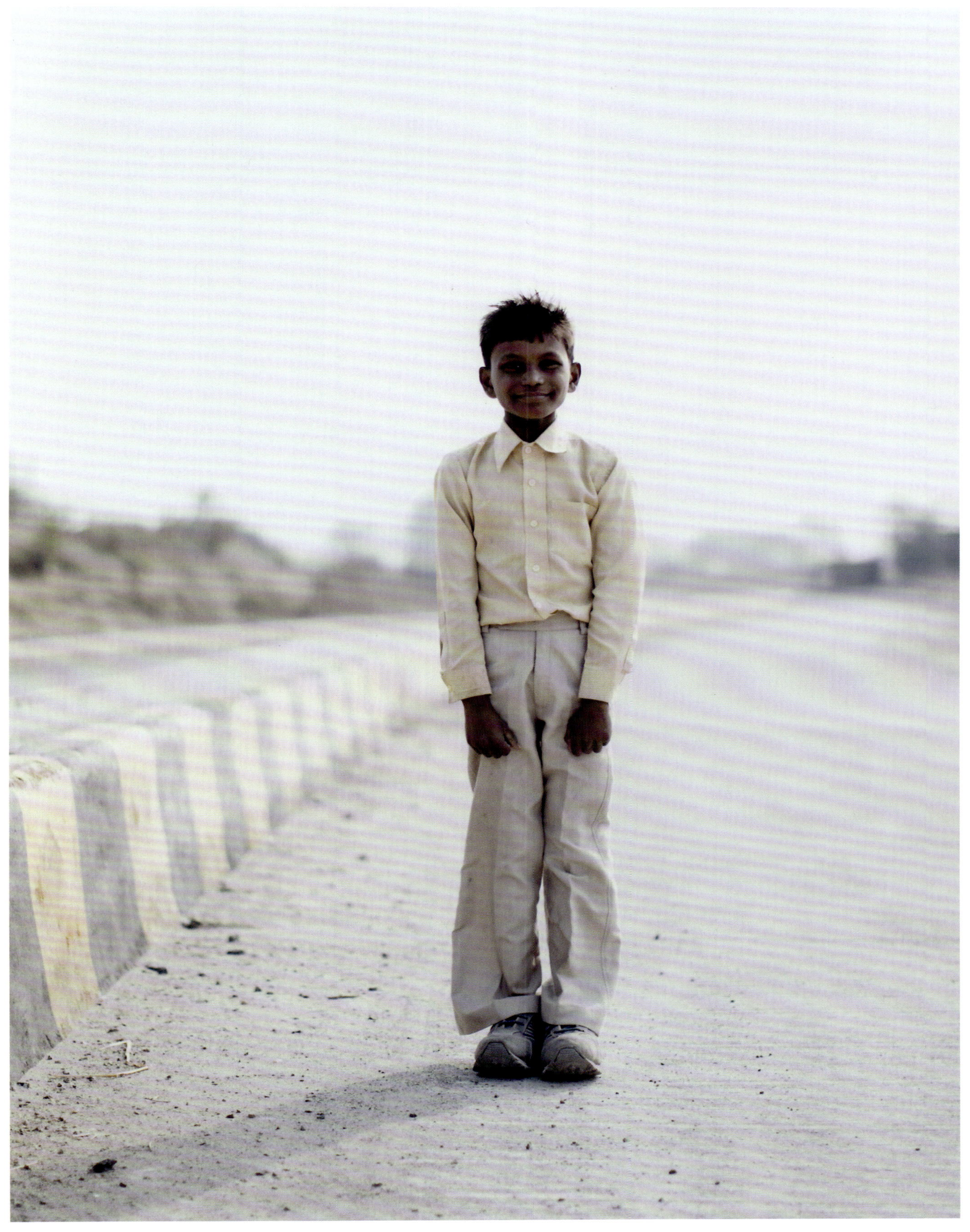

TOM SHAW
VIJAY
FROM THE SERIES *THE ROAD*
FEBRUARY 2011

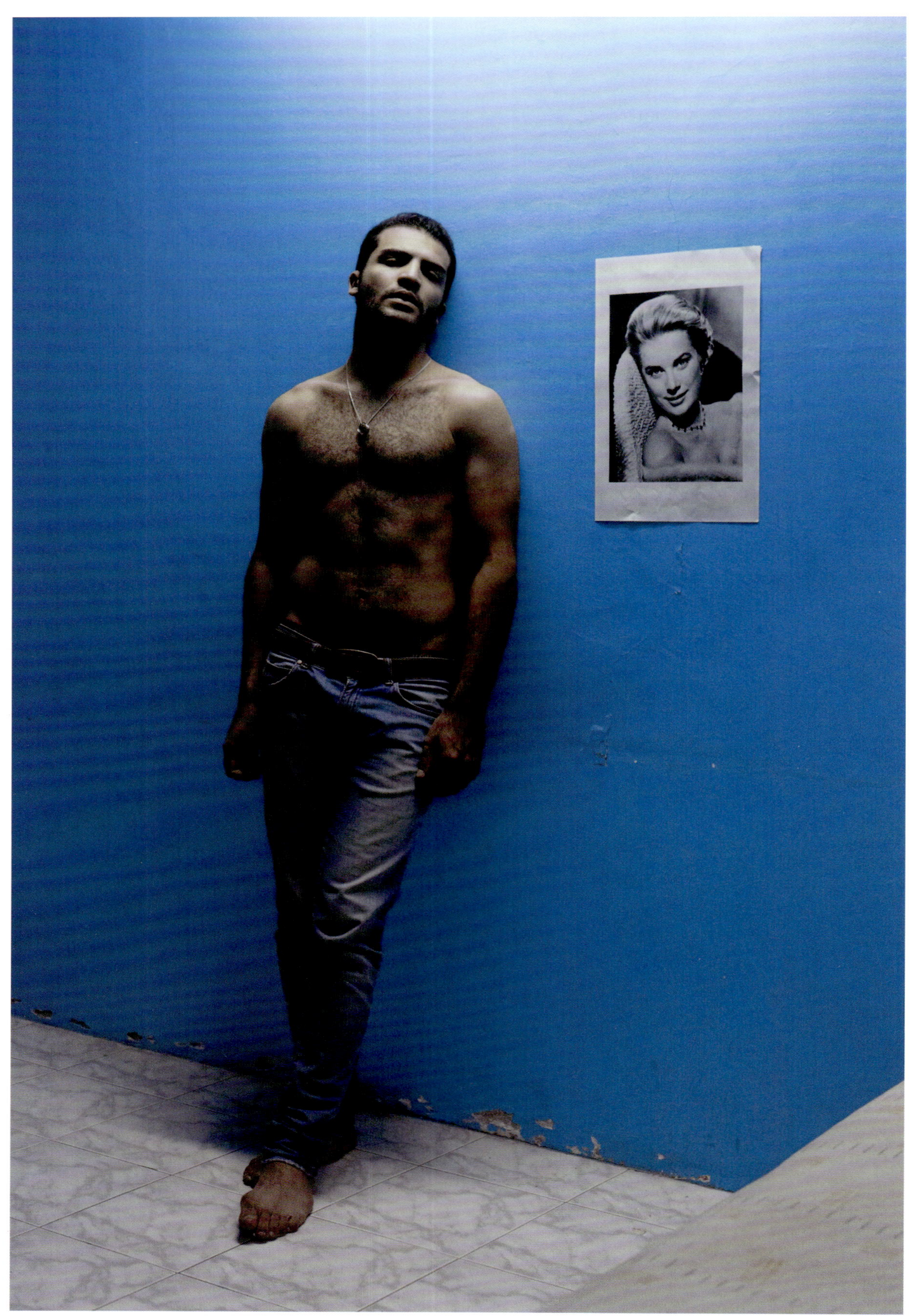

JOSEPH HUBER
YOUNG MAN IN HIS ROOM
FROM THE SERIES *FROM HER*
JANUARY 2010

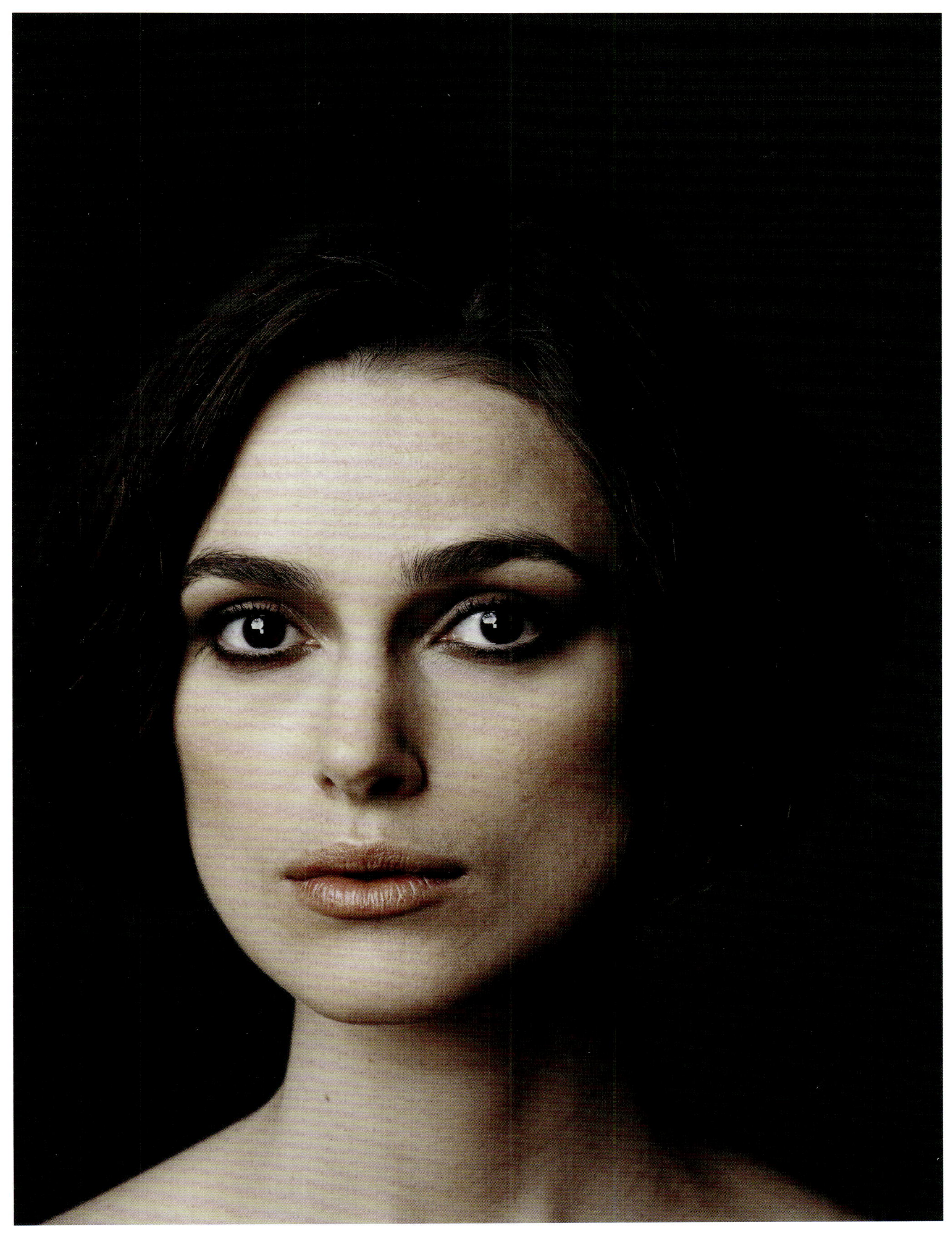

MICHAEL BIRT
KEIRA KNIGHTLEY
DECEMBER 2010

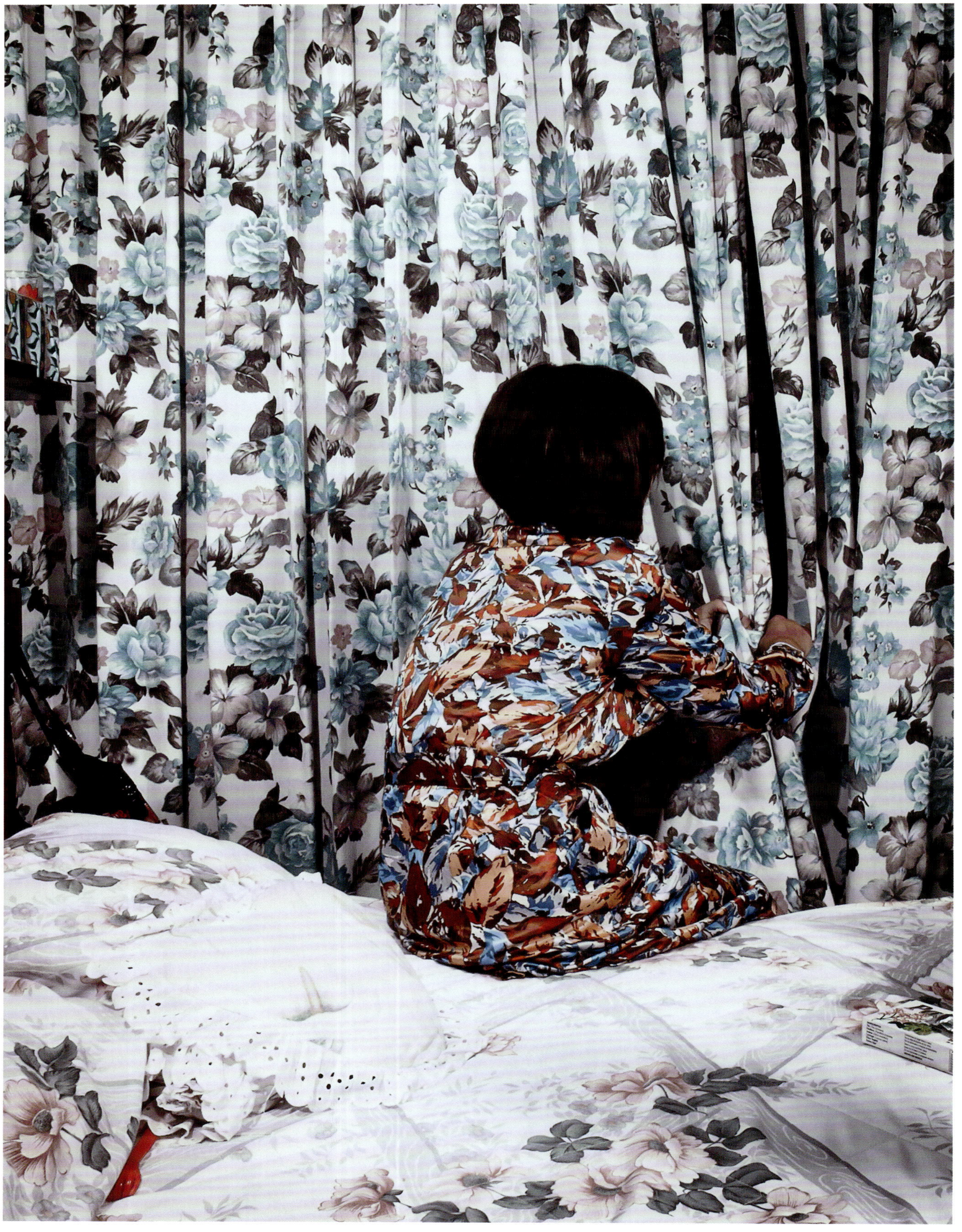

ROBERTO TONDOPO
FLOWER GARDEN
DECEMBER 2010

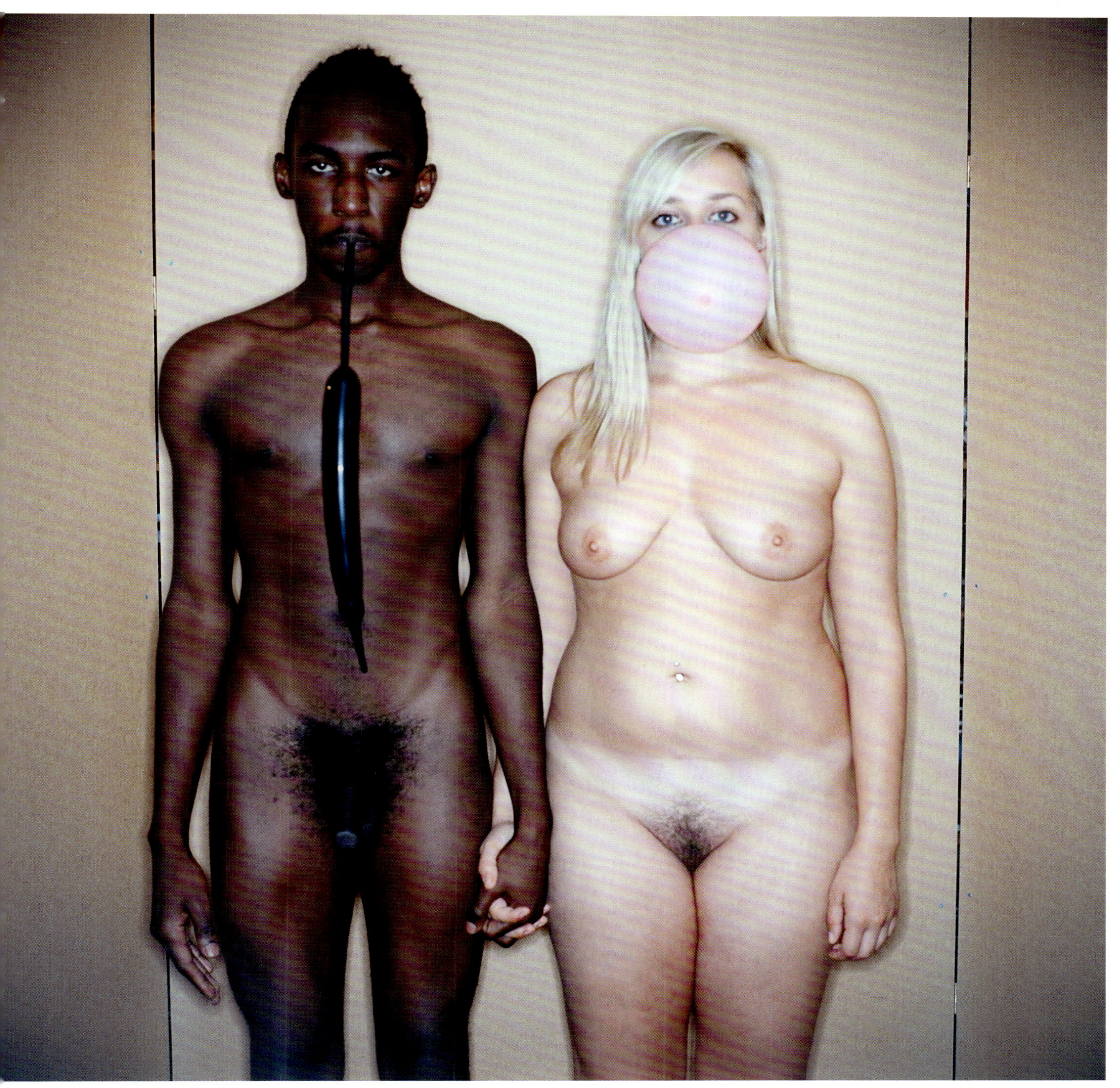

JULIAN BAKER
INFLATE
FROM THE SERIES *SKINTONES*
AUGUST 2010

LIST OF EXHIBITORS